A late wor
2014, the poli
heating up an
Democrats - w .... news. However,
more and more, it was evident to me that what was being said
(although maybe truthful) lacked greater substance.

For example, the performance of Hillary Clinton as
Secretary of State during the Benghazi debacle was shameful,
with cowardice and politics displayed! However, no one
including Democrats, Republicans, or news media Moguls, ever
mentioned or made an issue of what we were doing and why we
were there in the first place! Libya had not attacked us, nor was
Libya an enemy. As a result, Khadafy was killed, but why?

This incident followed in the footsteps of Obama and
Hillary having orchestrated a prolonged attack on our Mideast
ally, Egypt, which was a peace buffer (installed by former Pres.
Jimmy Carter), helping to protect Israel from the attacks and
incursions of the Palestinian terror group Hamas! Hamas is
owned by the Muslim Brotherhood, which by the way, is
supported by President Obama. Again, the question: Why did we
attack Egypt and Libya? To my knowledge, none of these actions
were authorized by Congress!

The point is that during the time-frame of my writing,
there are subjects now surfacing that had not been mentioned
during the initial writing period, such as Rudolph Giuliana
commenting that he doesn't believe that Obama loves America!
This is also, in my opinion, made clear in my chapter on Obama
and his "Inner Circle" of friends.

The Washington Weasels Association

By Claude Gray

A book of stories, deeds and misdeeds of some of our nation's highest officials, with the facts and history of these actions beginning in 1959 and continuing through early 2015. Even with the reader's familiarity with much of this material, readers will not find it boresome, but instead, *truthful winds from different directions.*

First Publishing: March 2015

http://claudegray.com/
claudegray1@aol.com

For inquiries, write or call:
11323 County Rd., 2116 North
Henderson, TX 75652
903-649-3205

INSTANTPUBLISHER.COM

Collierville, Tennessee

Contents

The Washington Weasels Association
(A Non-Exclusive Club)

*An association primarily composed of elected incumbents in Congress who are comfortable in their positions, who vote naively and are no longer effective; and their staffs, Cabinet members, certain reporters, journalists, and those in prominent positions who are deemed to be weasel-like. Such individuals are hereby involuntarily inducted as members of **The Washington Weasels Association**!*

The Washington Weasels Association

Politicians are a lot like cockroaches! It ain't so much what they eat up or tote off; it's what they walk across, fall into, and mess up!

-The Honorable late and great storyteller and humorist, Judge Joe Bob Murphy) - Nacogdoches, Texas

FOREWORD

This book is simply written with a *tell it like it is* flavor, with no respect to political correctness, and is unbiased as far as race, religion, or party! If it seems that the book is not complimentary to today's Democratic politicians, that's true! In the opinions of many folks (not only mine), there are too many *shaky politicians* sheltered under the umbrella of a Democratic Party which has become a party that Harry Truman, himself, would probably not tolerate or be a part of!

But, we also don't cut the Republicans any slack, either! There are far too many *Fat-Cat* politicians (Democrats and Republicans) sitting around in Washington with their fortunes made and their foremost thoughts are not of the safety, security, and the right direction of this country, but how to maintain the comfort, dignity, and prestige of their elected seats in Congress!

Without any doubt, we need more members of Congress who are *movers and shakers* and who stand strong, rather than boasting of an ability to reach across the aisle!

Although a lot of the material and thoughts of this book were written from memory, a great amount was selected from reputable, general news sources and the Internet. But, naturally, our comments and content will always be as truthful as possible, but in no case, are to be considered sworn testimony, and they are our opinion only.

Now, this being said, I am a registered Democrat. And, were I to have political icons, they would surely be the late presidents, Harry Truman and Ronald Reagan. I was 12 years old when Mr. Truman became president. Just a few years later, I joined the U.S. Navy in 1950 and served aboard an oil tanker - the USS Cacapon - mostly off the coast of Korea and in the South Pacific. I remember Harry Truman as a *rock solid straight shooter* who remained that way until he died on December 26, 1972.

If what I have read is true, when Truman's second term as president was over and he left the White House to his successor, General Dwight D. Eisenhower, he and his wife, the First Lady, Margaret Truman, rented a trailer to pull behind his 1951 Ford and drove back to their home in Independence, Missouri. *(A far cry from the huge 707 airliners now needed to transport ex-presidents, with their Secret Service agents, and throngs of staff, secretaries, office space, and their unending perks for life, all paid for by the taxpayers!)*

And, again, I believe it would be safe to say that Harry Truman would have very little to do with the current crop of politicians who call themselves Democrats in Congress, or with the presidency today, for that matter.

Also, I believe that while some presidents do play loosely with the truth, Harry Truman and Ronald Reagan never lied! It just didn't seem to have been a part of their make-up. However, lying and evading the truth have been prevalent by politicians and even presidents, going back many years in our nation's history.

During the years I lived in Nashville, I often visited the historical *Hermitage*, the home of our former President, Andrew Jackson. The *Hermitage* is an interesting place for the Nashville Chamber of Commerce to use as a promotion to tourists, but the long deceased President Andrew Jackson broke his pledge and promise to the Cherokee Indians. He made a solemn promise to the Cherokees (with the tribe's headquarters located east of Gatlinburg, Tennessee, just over the line in North Carolina), *that as long as the sun rises, and the rivers shall flow, this will be your home and your land!*

Not long afterwards, he sent in the U.S. Army and kicked my Great-Great Grandmas and Great-Great Grandpappys' rear-ends all those hundreds of miles to the eastern edge of Oklahoma, where they were settled in the area of what is now Tahlequah, which became the headquarters of the Cherokee Indian Nation. That journey is known as *The Trail of Tears.*

This leads to an interesting subject concerning the Indians' lifestyles and their manner of housekeeping. With some of the Indian tribes being nomadic in nature, and with their tribes and families on the move, littering, as we know it, by the Indians was virtually unknown out on the open prairies. The early mountain men in the West always claimed that when one of the Plains Indian tribes - Sioux, Kiowa, Cheyenne, etc. - even after camping for several weeks in a location, folded up their teepees and moved to a new hunting ground, one could hardly tell they had been there! No debris or odors.

On the other hand, when a typical wagon train of 20 or 30 covered wagons filled with settlers heading west from St. Louis camped overnight and left the next morning, the campgrounds would usually be cluttered with trash and would stink up the whole prairie! *Who would have thought that the Indian demographics would have had the cleaner lifestyles? And, with no EPA bureaucrats around)!*

Driving in my native East Texas, you might notice that the shoulders of our smaller county roads are covered with wrappers from just about every hamburger, fried chicken, and fast-food joint around. But, that's just our East Texas demographics of which I'm honored to be a part! *Rednecks, Wetbacks, Coonasses (Cajuns), and Black folks!*

Most folks would say that it's just a matter of demographics. And, if we think that demographics don't matter, just take a trip from northern Oklahoma up through Kansas, Iowa, and Nebraska, where the folks, for the most part, are of German or Polish origin, there won't even be a cigarette butt on the street! Most definitely, demographics matter!

The Washington Weasels Association

(Preamble)

From 1950 through 1954 I served in the U.S. Navy, then discharged, sold cars in Houston, and sang in beer-joints. In 1959, I got a job as a country music disc jockey in Meridian, Mississippi. I also started recording and had several *Top Ten* hits on the Billboard country music charts. Down through the years I was fortunate to have a number of Billboard top ten chart hits on Mercury, Columbia, Decca/MCA, and other record labels.

At the same time, I had my first experiences in covering a few stories in the Middle Mississippi area for WWL Radio, a CBS affiliate out of New Orleans. In 1962 I moved to Nashville and started working the road and also performing very regularly on the Grand Ole Opry. However, I have to say that the job and experience of being a news reporter is addictive. I had an offer to join the news staff at

WWL, but country music, the Opry and being an entertainer took first place in my life! But, through the years, I have tried to keep abreast of news, world affairs, and the treatment by our news media.

The Kennedy Assassination

(The Probable Suspects and Killers)

Presently, the Kennedy Assassination is a subject that at this writing is once again in the news, with at least two new books released, and as always, awash with theories. With all of this said, included here are what seem to me to be the most logical and truthful reasons for the assassination, and the foremost persons involved.

It was an unforgettable morning of November 22, 1963. Along with country rock singer Carl Perkins, I had checked into a Motel 6 about 1:30 AM that morning in the small town of Troy, Ohio. Carl and I were close friends and had driven from Nashville to Troy for a show with *Grand Ole Opry* acts George Morgan, Del Wood, and the Duke of Paducah.

When we arose about 11:00 AM, we turned on the television and heard the devastating news that President Kennedy had been shot in Dallas, Texas. Not long after that tragic news, we heard the final report that he was in fact, dead on arrival at Parkland

Hospital in Dallas.

That evening we had a fairly large crowd at the high school auditorium and the Duke of Paducah delivered a very moving eulogy that paid all of our respects to our President, without casting a sense of gloom on the show.

The next day, we all drove to Toledo and had a large crowd there. On the way back to Nashville, we kept the radio tuned to WSM, the 50,000 watt NBC affiliate in Nashville, for an uninterrupted, live broadcast almost all day. What with the search for Oswald, the alleged suspect in the assassination of Kennedy, and the President's body having been flown back to Washington, it was an active day!

During the *Live on the Scene* NBC broadcast, there was the procession of moving the President's body in the wagon, with the saddled black horse following. A large part of the broadcast day was filled with conversations by various reporters, and I might mention NBC's Sander Vanocur, who had a conversation with a high Catholic official - a Cardinal – who asked the Cardinal if the millions of prayers from Catholics around the world praying for the President's soul would have any effect for his salvation? Surprisingly, at least to me, the Cardinal said no. He said that a person's soul would be judged entirely by that person's life and actions here on earth.

(With the reader's permission, I would like to expound a little further regarding Carl Perkins for those who might not be totally familiar with him. Carl came from a dirt-scrabble Tennessee farm family, including Luther Perkins, who was the lead guitar player for Johnny Cash, and familiarized the Thump-Thump sound that we remember so well, as a part of the Johnny Cash sound.)

At the time, even with Carl having written and recorded the monster hit, *Blue Suede Shoes,* I never realized the fame and even idol-like adoration that that he had overseas in England and Europe! The *Beatles* were not around at this time (in 1963), but later after 1965, and years later, from time to time, the Beatles would fly Carl over to England and pay him large amounts to just hang around and maybe "buddy-buddy", and give them a few tips! Elvis Presley later recorded *Blue Suede Shoes* and of course, it was also a big hit, but to the Beatles, Carl was always *The Man!*

Carl, Elvis, Johnny Cash, Roy Orbison, and Jerry Lee Lewis all began and were all a part of the *Sun Records* family in Memphis, started by Sam Phillips, who passed away some several years ago. Carl Perkins passed away in 1997 in a Memphis hospital from a long term illness.

I just barely remember that Sam Phillips (Sun Records) sold Elvis's recording contract to RCA Victor Records around 1956, - I believe - for $40,000! That, of course, would be just pocket change now, but back then, it was real money.

With a final remembrance of Carl, I will also always remember the first tour in the fall of 1962, with Carl, Jimmy Dean, Patsy Cline, and me, for the great Iowa country music promoter, D. C. "Smokey" Smith, from Des Moines. Regrettably, Smokey passed away February 3, 2014. The five day tour ended in Burlington, Iowa. Carl, myself, Jimmy Dean, and Patsy were sitting backstage while the musicians were packing up the equipment. Carl and Jimmy were both talented boozers and Carl had his usual bottle of Jim Beam with him. Jimmy Dean was doing his best to *help out,* and Patsy and me had a "toddy," just to be sociable!

Carl had his guitar and was doing a recitation of a sad song he had just written called *"21".* The song was a "hit" by country singer Bill Anderson. Patsy started crying and said, *Damn you, Carl, don't sing them kinda songs, you know I can't stand 'em!* Carl said, *I'm sorry, Patsy, I won't do it no more!*

Jimmy Dean said, *That's one hell of a song, Carl, and I believe I'll have just another touch of that Beam, and a drop or two of sprang water.* Carl said, *O.K. on the Beam, but we ain't got nothin' but plain 'ole tap water!* Jimmy said, *Well, I'll take a chance, and hope it don't rust my pipes!*

Carl then started another recitation about an old colored gentleman who was fishing in a hole of water in a creek where there had just been a baptism! The old gentleman was saying, *You know, Lord, we sho' don't mind that fine young preacher havin' a baptism in our fishin' hole! He's doin' good, Lord, and gettin' rid of lots of sin! And, Lord, I just know these perch is gonna taste a lot's more sweetuh, after they swim thru where you been!* Patsy burst out, *Damn you, Carl Perkins, don't you listen at all? I told you what them kinda songs do to me!*

Carl said, *I'm sorry, Patsy...I won't do it no more.* Patsy Cline, Jimmy Dean, and Carl Perkins all had big hearts. They were friends of mine.

The Probable Suspects and Killers

In Dallas and Washington, things were in a total uproar. Vice-President Lyndon B. Johnson had been sworn in as President almost immediately after the assassination by Judge Sarah Hughes aboard Air Force One, and there was already an investigative committee being formed to determine as to who the killer was, did he have help, etc.

As we all know today, this whole thing has been looked at and talked about in every possible way. Jack Ruby, (the manager of a strip joint) easily entered into the jail because he was well-known by most of the cops and is the one who shot Oswald, of course. All sorts of rumors have since floated around. Even exhuming Oswald's coffin in the 1980's (to make sure that the body was in fact, Oswald, and it was), the verdict remains the same! That Oswald was the lone killer. Maybe?

Well, if I had been a paid journalist on the payroll of a large newspaper, magazine, or news organization, I believe I would have headed south to the Dominican Republic! Here's why:

Three important pieces of information that help to draw a conclusion as to the more than probable reasons and persons involved in the killing of President Kennedy:

1. On December 30, 1961, President Raphael Trujillo of the Dominican Republic was slain, execution style, in the early morning while traveling along a beach front road.

2. In 1977, a book titled *It Didn't Start at Watergate* was written by a well-known writer in Washington, Victor Lasky. The book wasn't written to excuse President Richard Nixon for his indiscretions, but to show that covert and possibly illegal actions have been conducted and condoned by almost all presidents.

The book describes as how on December 30, 1961, in the early morning, the president of the Dominican Republic, Raphael Trujillo, was traveling in a blue Chevrolet with his chauffer along a beach front road for a visit with his mistress. Suddenly, a car pulls alongside, men inside open fire and Mr. Trujillo is slain! It was found that although the CIA was interested to a small extent in the Dominican Republic's affairs, *which President Kennedy did know about and condone*, he did not order any action so drastic.

However, the weapons used reportedly came from the CIA and were M-1 rifles. Officially, the CIA only admits: With respect to Trujillo's assassination on May 30, 1961, the CIA had 'no active part' but had a 'faint connection' with the groups who in fact did do it.

3. In the year of 1993, (in a news report) it was reported by major news media in the U.S. that a high Cuban government official made the statement, that *there were three people responsible for the assassination of President John F. Kennedy. One was a Cuban, one was a Venezuelan, and the third person was from the Dominican Republic.*

Importantly, the personal aide of Trujillo (who *would have* had a motive or desire for revenge against President Kennedy for killing his boss and friend) was mentioned. Certainly, something to think about and seriously consider!

It seems we all liked President Kennedy. He had a nice family, and he had all the class, grooming, and prestige that wealth and a political family can bestow. With the strength and support of his brother Robert, and the entire country, he stood up to the

Russians and, at the least, arrived at a stalemate with them regarding the Cuban missile crisis. *(On a personal note, his brother, Robert, seemed to be the stronger of the two.)*

After Kennedy's death, we all watched as his wife, the former First Lady Jacquelyn Kennedy, graciously lived her life, and raised her two children, John-John, and Caroline, in an exemplary manner. Her eventual second marriage to the rich Greek shipping magnate Aristotle Onassis never diminished the love and respect that we as a country felt for her. Of her two children, John was killed in a small plane crash, and Caroline never entered politics. Recently, as of this writing, she did accept the position of being our Ambassador to Japan. I think most of us would agree that this was a fine appointment.

We should also recognize and give credit to the guy who probably more than anyone, was responsible for the peaceful and successful ending to the Cuban crisis. That would surely be John Scali of *ABC News,* who was stationed in Washington, D.C. and was trusted by the personnel in the Russian Embassy. Mr. Scali literally brokered the agreement by going back and forth between the White House and the Russian Embassy. John Scali should be more extensively thanked and remembered.

President Lyndon B. Johnson

(Shortly after this book was written, but prior to being published, the movie "Selma" has been produced and released. This movie undoubtedly will parallel some of the events which are mentioned in this writing and in the chapter "President Lyndon B. Johnson". From the very small amount of footage that has been shown - only in promo ads, - it would appear there is a possibility that the movie just might depict Mr. King as espousing demonstrations that were not necessarily peaceful. Let us hope not, because it just wasn't his way!)

Vice President Lyndon B. Johnson came into office as President in the aftermath and turmoil following the death of President John F. Kennedy. He had been a powerful Democratic senator from Texas and had a sort of checkered past with stories of voting discrepancies and such. Well, Ole Lyndon might have been a *Redneck* but he was easy-going and he had that great and most valuable asset, *the Endearment Factor*!

President Johnson inherited some big, leftover problems - one being the growing Vietnam War which former President Dwight D. Eisenhower actually initiated, and which President Kennedy had joined in. This war was a *Southeast Asian Treaty Organization (SEATO)* exercise and the United States was a member. Mr. Johnson didn't back off or hesitate. If we remember, the Gulf of Tonkin incident, where a North Vietnamese torpedo boat supposedly attacked one of our destroyers, was the excuse for us to officially get in the war with both feet!

Then, there was also the huge Civil Rights movement (which caught fire under President Kennedy) sweeping across the country under the direction and leadership of the Reverend Martin Luther King. Reverend King was the charismatic leader that maybe comes along once in a lifetime.

And, no doubt, Reverend King had the right ingredients with which to work. The entire country, outside of the South, was being caught up almost to the point of being mesmerized, with the Southern culture and way of life coming under attack from all points: North, East, West, and even in a limited way, the South, all joining in with an almost concentrated effort to end the many years of segregation. There was one purpose: to make sure that all folks are treated equally, at least in the eyes of the government, regarding entrances to restaurants, housing availability, public transportation and other things that we live by in the USA.

The 1964 Presidential Election

Going into the 1964 elections, President Johnson was only a minimally popular president. As well as we remember, the economy was reasonably good, but the country was in a turbulent mood. The Republican nominee was Arizona Senator Barry Goldwater, who was a fairly likeable man and a solid conservative, but as always, with Republican presidential candidates, they often tend to be bland, colorless men, and will literally bore the hell out of most voting blocks, and especially, the Black demographics!

Those demographics were not that much of a factor at that time, but they have drastically grown since the Voting Rights Act was passed in 1965, and are a *huge consideration* these days!

The Atomic war factor was something that many folks worried about then. We had just endured the Cuban Missile Crisis and folks were still on edge, so President Johnson took advantage of the situation by promoting the scenario that he, as president, was the best person to keep a firm hand on the *trigger of the atomic bomb*. There are those of us who remember the Democratic Party commercials showing the picture of the little girl with an atom bomb mushroom cloud behind her!

Republican Senator Barry Goldwater did lose the 1964 Presidential election to Democratic President Lyndon B. Johnson, even with a nationally televised magnificent speech by Ronald Reagan just a few days prior to the election that almost turned the election to Goldwater!

A small amount of that *Endearment Factor* would have made the difference! However, that speech did bring the profile of Ronald Reagan into prominence, helping to make him a future nominee.

In 1965, President Johnson signed into effect the Civil Rights Law. And, of course, that was a good thing, and should have been. However, a great *feel good* mistake was made by voiding the **literacy test requiremen**t, which effectively removed the need of any intelligence or knowledge in order to vote! Of course, we should all have the right to vote intelligently! No disagreement there. But should persons having no informed idea of the **quality** of candidates, or any **knowledge at all** about a candidate, be able to, let's say, **blindly vote**? *Such is what has helped to keep the African continent dark for these hundreds of years!*

Lately, some states have passed their own voter ID photo laws but the liberal Democrats,

NAACP, and Civil Rights leaders are squealing, saying these voters are being disenfranchised, and *the Reverend Al Sharpton and his Choir are doing new versions of the St. Vitus Dance!* One Circuit Judge in Pennsylvania recently, as of this writing, struck down that state's voter ID law with the statement that: *The voter's photo ID might not be convenient to the voter.* Do you get it folks? *(From this judge, we have a great example of a politically correct, well-intentioned road to destruction!)*

Notably, in 1965, as we said, the year when the Voting Act was passed, those particular demographics were not large enough to greatly affect the outcome of an election. *However, at this time, our country is dangerously at the point where those demographics can and do matter! Let's be aware that our country is not as impervious to such destructive abuse as we might wish.*

The Civil Rights and Vietnam War Protests

Without a doubt, the Vietnam War protests - coupled with the Civil Rights Movement - the year of 1965 set into motion the greatest movement of demonstrations and protests (mainly across the Deep South) that our country has ever witnessed or endured.

So, what with the Civil Rights struggle and the building opposition to the Vietnam War, President Johnson had his plate full! It became the refrain of the times, and the days of the long-haired Hippies,

"Hey, Hey, Hey, LBJ, How Many Kids Did You Kill today? So let the demonstrations begin"!

They came! They hitch-hiked, traveled in old school buses, vans, old Volkswagens, in groups, singles, college students, professors, all happy and anxious to get to where the great gatherings and demonstrations would be getting underway! To Selma, Birmingham, Tuscaloosa, Memphis, Little Rock, and all the memorable moments and places destined to be a part of our history!

And, of course there was usually an adequate number of Black folks, drawn from the local populations (for a proper "mix") to be included in the loads of passengers on the vehicle. (In those days, Blacks were properly called *Negroes or Colored Folks*, with the use of the term *Blacks* being added at the suggestion of the Reverend Jesse Jackson, in the late 1960s). And finally, the term *African-American* came into usage sometime later. *However, for the sake of appearances, there had to be, indeed, a good mix of Black folks among the Freedom Riders and protesters!*

They came! From Boston, Minneapolis, Denver, New York and San Francisco! For the college students, it was a time of getting acquainted, getting to know each other, being together, just talking and surely *falling in love*, and then, *making love with those special ones who agree and are on the great mission, as the rest of us.*

And, the great song writers and Folk singers and musicians, Pete Seeger, Bob Dillon, the

Kingston trio, Peter, Paul, and Mary, were all heroes, and icons to cling to! All a part of a movement where *the Times are a' changin' and the Answers are Blowing in the Wind.*

The saying that *good demonstrators will march in any demonstrations that will have them* is certainly true! A few little hardships never bothered the confirmed demonstrators! Just the excitement of being involved was enough in those truly glorious days!

Naturally, as we might expect, with minimum bathroom facilities, living conditions for the students, Freedom Riders, and professors on the old buses and vans, caused the atmosphere to be a little less sanitary than desired, but more flavorful! So, at frequent stops at convenience stores, the most ordered merchandise was paper towels, underarm deodorant, and Air-wick!

For the next three years or so, some of the greatest and most monumental events in history, took place with the Civil Rights and anti-war protests. Who could ever forget the long 120 mile march by the thousands of demonstrators from Selma, Alabama, to Montgomery? Or, the Police Chief, "Bull" Connors in Birmingham with the police dogs and fire hoses? And finally, who could forget the federal government, forcing the desegregation and integration of the schools and the universities in Little Rock, Arkansas, and Jackson, Miss.? *And of course, the sad spectacle of four small children killed in the church bombing in Birmingham?*

And, there were the African-Americans summoning up courage to move from the back of the bus to the front when seats were available! The restaurant owner in Atlanta, Lester Maddox, who carried the axe handle to forcibly prevent any Black Folks from entering without his permission*! (As it turned out, Lester Maddox was elected governor of Georgia after those episodes, and ironically, became one of the best liked governors in Georgia history. He appointed more African-Americans to prominent positions in his administration, than all governors before him!)*

But in the end, LBJ couldn't overcome the unpopular Vietnam War syndrome, and the very liberal Senator George McGovern from South Dakota, somehow attracted such a large following, that President Johnson decided not to try for re-election in 1968.

President Richard Nixon

President Richard Nixon was actually a very good president. He had been the Vice President under former General and President, Dwight D. Eisenhower, and so he had the necessary knowledge and experience needed to handle the presidency. However, a situation known as *Watergate* derailed his presidency. That event was in 1972 (40+ years ago) and most of us have heard of, and some remember it; but even then, definite details were murky.

Mr. Nixon was forced to resign due to charges of lying concerning Watergate in 1974, halfway through his second term, and Vice-President Gerald Ford took over the reins of the presidency. As if possibly pre-arranged, the new president, Gerald Ford, swiftly pardoned Nixon for his sins. As we said, Richard Nixon was a good President and in the last few months prior to his leaving the presidency, he took a trip to China and opened diplomatic doors that had been closed for years. Mr. Nixon was also putting into motion the final touches on negotiating the ending of the Vietnam War.

Richard Nixon, facing impeachment, resigned from office on August 9, 1974. He is the only president to have resigned in the history of the United States.

President Gerald R. Ford

The controversial pardon that President Ford gave former President Richard Nixon angered a lot of Americans, but in the end, it was viewed as being a good thing. It was a full and free pardon for all offenses that Mr. Nixon may have committed against the United States.

Actually, President Ford had a very active Presidency during the short two year period he had inherited from Nixon. The Vietnam War was brought to a close in a *good ol' boy* sort of way with neither the North Vietnamese, nor the U.S. and its allies claiming victory. (Just sort of *We're all tired, so let's stop shootin' and go home for a while.)*

In May 1975, an international incident occurred when the U.S. merchant ship *Mayagüez* was seized by Cambodian communist Khmer Rouge forces in the Gulf of Thailand. President Ford didn't hesitate. He sent in the Marines, and after some fierce fighting, all 39 members of the ship were released,

In 1975, I believe, President Ford put a freeze on all prices and wages to stop inflation. Writing from memory, I think the freeze lasted for some months.

In the 1976 election, President Ford beat out Ronald Reagan for the Republican presidential nomination, and faced the former Governor of Georgia, Jimmy Carter, for the presidency. Jimmy won the race by about two million votes.

President Jimmy Carter

(Star Member of the Washington Weasels Association)

He came up out of the State of Georgia in 1974, a former member of the Georgia Legislature and serving out the last year or so of his term as Governor. He surfaced in the Bay area of San Francisco, California, in late 1974 and was already working and campaigning for votes in the up and coming Democratic primaries for the office of President of the United States. At the time, I was staying temporarily in Berkeley for a few months and working around the West Coast. One thing I do remember about living in Berkeley - especially about 5 blocks from the college, - was, that if you drove an old Volkswagen, or any older car, you were ok to park it on the side of the street. But if you had a new expensive car, (I had a Cadillac) in order to be safe, you better park it inside; otherwise, some well-meaning college student or hippie passing by, - not meaning any harm of course - was liable to take a knife or such, and mess up a good paint job!

Those were good days. There were two popular night clubs in Sacramento where I appeared sort of regularly. The 50,000 watt AM Country music Radio Station KRAK in Sacramento covered all of Northern and Central California and Country music had good radio exposure. (This all changed a few years later when talk radio came along and almost all AM radio stations changed formats from country music to talk.)

Rush Limbaugh, one of the pioneers in talk radio, started his first days in radio in Sacramento, I believe, on KRAK. I never had the opportunity to meet Limbaugh, but he's always been, I'm sure, one heck of a nice guy! From what I understand, more than one cop said he was one of the nicest guys they ever had in their patrol wagons! *(Just kidding, Rush!)*

Well, ole Jimmy Carter was running for president. And he was a likeable guy! As a *peanut farmer (*their family business*),* he, as the stories went, managed to screw that up successfully, until his brother Billy came and rescued the situation, and brought in some good crops of peanuts! As to Jimmy's performance as Governor, his record may have been nothing to write home about, but it must have been good enough that no red flags were raised!

But when it came to campaigning for President, he was one hell of a promoter, and knew what to say! And he had the *Endearment Factor!* Who can forget the television coverage of the draining of a stock pond behind Jimmy's house, with Jimmy holding a big bass and daughter, little Amy, perched in the small tree?

The Christian Coalition in the Carolinas and

other parts of the South at that time was one of the biggest voting blocs in the country! *Somewhat naive in some respects, but good folks! If the rest of us were of their moral character, we could throw away our locks and keys. Amen?* Well, Ol' Jimmy immediately went right to their *nerve centers, hearts and pulpits,* with the statement, *"I Will Nevuh Lie To You"*, which of course, was a *World Class Whopper,* and stood unequaled until *Bill Clinton and Barack Obama* came along!

In the Presidential election of 1976, Jimmy Carter won the race over Gerald Ford by about two million votes! And the next four years were a disorderly course, to say it mildly, of *A Seemingly Naive Trip of Unintentional Destruction.*

Jimmy Carter assumed the Presidency on January 20, 1977 and got right to the business at hand! *The business of giving away the Panama Canal*! He had promised that he would turn over (*give*) the Canal to Panama, for whatever reasons, no one could see. Perhaps Mr. Carter thought that it would be a magnanimous gesture from the President and the United States and he would be viewed that way by Panama and the rest of the world!

Well, more than anything, it seemed to be viewed by Panama as a "stupid" action in the sense that we (the U.S.) had bought the land from Panama, built the Canal, were managing the Canal and paying for the upkeep, plus giving Panama a portion of the income! They never had it so good! *Oh well, good intentions!*

The Shah of Iran

In late 1943, The President of the United States, Franklin D. Roosevelt, with British Prime Minister Winston Churchill, and Russian leader Joseph Stalin, met in Tehran, Iran to formulate an agreement called the *Tehran Agreement* and plan for further actions against Germany. Supposedly, hotel and living accommodations were not good in Tehran, so the leaders all stayed at the Russian Embassy.

It is said, (with fairly reliable information), that the *Shah* had managed to secretly get a message and a request to Roosevelt for his support with the following problem: The *Shah* was concerned that Russia, which borders Iran, had moved massive amounts of personnel, troops, and equipment, etc., into Iran. The *Shah* was not objecting to having the Russians in his country, but was very worried that at the close of World War II, Russia might not move their personnel and equipment out of Iran and back across the border into Russia.

The content of the message and request was that; if Roosevelt would *strongly request* that Stalin sign an agreement that they *(the Russians)* would move their troops, etc., out of Iran at the war's end; then Iran and the United States would have an undying friendship! FDR did honor the *Shah's* request, the Russians did agree to leave Iran at the end of the war, and did honor the agreement! *The Undying Eternal Friendship between Iran and the United States endured for about 34 years, until President Jimmy Carter came along.*

On December 31, 1977, President Carter with his wife, Rosalind, was honored with a State dinner in Tehran by the son (now young *Shah*), and during the event, the *young Shah (Mohammad Reza Pahlavi)* again offered a toast to the *"Unshakeable link of friendship between our two countries that has endured so many, many years!"* Carter accepted the honor and the toast!

Not too long after that dinner, President Jimmy Carter back-stabbed the Shah, and with his human rights team, promoted an untrue image of the Shah as a tyrannical despot. *(Actually, by comparison of Mideastern leaders, the Shah was a very benevolent ruler. Women were no longer forced to wear veils and alcoholic drinks could be consumed in restaurants, etc.).*

At the same time, Carter fomented and helped to promote an insurrection led by an insurrectionist, Ahmadinejad who was a rebel and a Muslim extremist. As the crowds grew in the streets, the pressure grew on the Shah to step down from the seat of power that he and his family had held for so many years.

In ill health, suffering from cancer, the Shah was unable to resist and forced to relinquish his power and the Carter backed insurrectionist, Ahmadinejad, took over the government. At the same time, the Ayatollah Khomeini, who had been banned from Iran by the Shah, was living in France, and Carter opened the door for his return to Iran! *If Jimmy Carter had never known a really cruel tyrannical Muslim leader, he surely met one in the person of the Ayatollah Khomeini!* The coming years of living under the government ruled by the Ayatollah Khomeini and Ahmadinejad were a Hell and Nightmare in Iran!

Sometime after relinquishing power, the Shah traveled to Mexico in order to try to enter the United States to get treatment for his cancer. Carter then displayed his Christian soul and compassion by refusing the Shah permission! The Shah then went back to the Mideast and finally passed away in Egypt. (*And, that great link of friendship of many, many years, between Iran and the U.S. also passed away, compliments of Jimmy Carter.*)

Shortly after Ahmadinejad assumed power, he double-crossed Carter and took control of the U.S. embassy, taking the U.S. embassy personnel (52) hostage. *Well, what to do now?*

To rescue 52 Americans held captive at the U.S. Embassy in Tehran on 24 April 1980 was a priority! An airlift operation that was launched (Carter insisted on directing the operation from the White House) ran into a lot of problems landing in the desert about fifty odd miles from Tehran and eight service men were killed when two of the aircraft (a helicopter and transport plane) crashed into each other and caught fire. The mission was aborted, but the humiliating and embarrassing publicity that ensued damaged American prestige around the world. The embassy hostages were released on the day (*actually at the exact time*) that Ronald Reagan took the oath and assumed the Presidency!

Carter seemed to lean favorably towards any individual or leader who had Socialist or Communist oriented views, such as the Sandinistas in Nicaragua who were Communist directed. It was tempting for Carter to back the Sandinistas due to President Somoza, who ruled in Nicaragua for about thirty years, being viewed as a dictator. So, Carter threw his support to the Sandinistas and Somoza was deposed.

(Much later and immediately after assuming the Presidency, President Ronald Reagan managed to help Mr. Somoza regain his leadership. President Reagan didn't want another Communist Country - such as Cuba - on our doorsteps in the Caribbean! This subject and operation is discussed more fully

later in the President Reagan chapter.)

Not too long after he assumed the presidency, Jimmy Carter signed a pardon for all Vietnam era draft dodgers, most of whom had moved to Canada and taken up residency there. Bill Clinton (who later became president after George H. Bush), was not technically a draft dodger, but a *draft evader*, in the sense that, even after being warned and requested to show up at the draft board, no warrants were ever issued for his arrest!

Carter's Disasters in Zimbabwe

Rhodesia was a very prosperous country. It was settled by white men in about 1891, (*and by this, we don't mean that it was settled in the face of Africans who were already living there; we mean that there was no established population already there.)* It was a land of marauding animals and isolated tribes of *"Bushmen"* with Zulus passing through now and then and raiding. The White settlers actually settled Rhodesia in ways somewhat similar to the establishment of our government here in America, with the difference being that any major problems or raiding attacks came from without Rhodesia, rather than from within, as compared to problems from the Indians who were already established in America, long before the white man arrived!

Rhodesia was rich in minerals, gold and

silver, and was a heavy exporter of farm products.

The settlers built huge plantations and farms, with a small percentage of the Africans, (Blacks) joining in and also having farms. With almost everyone having jobs, and prosperity abounding, it was only natural that Blacks from other countries in Africa would be moving in to Rhodesia not only for the jobs, but for the comparative safety and security which the country enjoyed. It was true that as the country grew, the White population and ownership of land and farms grew with the White farmers in the late 1960's owning and controlling about 90 percent of the land and properties, but making up only ten percent of the population! These figures are from Census polls taken from 1968 with a total population count of about 4 and a half million. *This was the situation when the great humanitarian, President Jimmy Carter arrived!*

Jimmy and his *Human Rights Crew* took a good look at Rhodesia, with the beauty, the abundance and prosperity of the country with its high employment and Africans (Blacks) waiting in line to enter Rhodesia where the jobs, security, and prosperity abounded, something that few countries in the African continent could or did offer. *But Jimmy never noticed that!* Jimmy noted that he didn't like a situation in a country where ten percent of the population, (the White folks), controlled 90 percent of the land! No matter that the Whites had founded and built the country into an example of safety and abundance that was the envy of Africa! *It Just Wasn't Right!*

As we said before, Rhodesia was blessed with minerals such as gold and silver. But it had something that was found in only one other country, Bolivia, I believe, *chrome!* Well, now! Carter's thoughts: *Let's put some hurt on Mr. Ian Smith and that White-ruled government... Never mind that they settled the country and have been in power since 1890!*

Carter had on hand a less than brilliant, Democratic Congressman from the Dallas, Texas area, Jim Mattox, and persuaded him to get enough Congressmen to join in and pass a Congressional resolution that U.S. manufacturers and companies could not buy chrome from Rhodesia, even though Bolivia did not have sufficient product to supply! Good going there Jimmy! *But, wait!* Where do our car manufacturers, buy chrome? O.K., from Russia! Fine! *But wait*, where does Russia buy its chrome? Well, from Rhodesia! Sure it costs us a little more to buy it from Russia, but hey, maybe we're sure puttin' some hurt on Mr. Smith and his government!

England, at that time, had a fairly moderate Prime Minister and Cabinet, and somehow (and I really have never known why), Carter was able to convince the Britons to join with him in expanding bans on farm products, chrome, and other necessities from Rhodesia. Eventually, under pressure from

Carter's regime in the U.S. and the British, President Ian Smith of Rhodesia agreed to turn over power to whoever Carter might have the option to select, but with the agreement including a strong condition that whoever assumed the seat of power would not molest or bother the plantations, farmers, and mining industry! This seemed reasonable to Carter. Any leader Carter would choose should know that the farms were the life blood of Rhodesia!

Throughout the history of Rhodesia, there had always been sporadic raids across the borders from other countries into Rhodesia, but the farmers were sturdy people and with the help of their neighbors, including Blacks and Whites, they always managed to handle the situations with minimum damage!

One of the more blood-thirsty raiders was a Communist working out of Mozambique. He raided and destroyed indiscriminately the farms and homes of both Blacks and Whites. His name was **Robert Mugabe.**

Who did Jimmy Carter select to assume the reins of power in Rhodesia? It really shouldn't surprise anyone! *President Jimmy Carter selected* **Robert Mugabe**, *the main robber and murderer, who had been raiding over the border from Mozambique for a number of years!* So, what had been a beautiful, prosperous country with great abundance is now (and has been for the last 35 years) a killing field, wracked with starvation, misery and poverty, with its people living in fear! *Shortly after Mugabe took power, the country's name was changed from Rhodesia to Zimbabwe.*

Mugabe still holds the seat of power after about 35 years. He nationalized the lands and farms which he used to distribute to buy votes and steal the elections! Most of the Whites have left the country, leaving virtually no stabilizing factors.

*(*Admittedly, the volume of details in this story may be somewhat varied, but the overall substance is quite accurate!)

Jimmy Carter was not re-elected for a second term. It is said, - reliably - that on the eve of the election, President Carter and Rosalind were flying home from a final campaign appearance in Seattle, and one of their aides came back to them and revealed to them that they had lost the election. In a late poll, they could not overcome Ronald Reagan! Accordingly, both Jimmy and Rosalind started crying!

For those who would like a fictionalized (but pretty true picture I believe), of the afterlife of the Carter - Rhodesian debacle, I would like to suggest a novel of fiction written by the South African writer Wilbur Smith, titled, "The Leopard Hunts In Darkness".

President Ronald Reagan

Ronald Reagan took the oath of office on January 20, 1981 and wasted little time in correcting some of the mistakes and utter mess left behind from the Carter regime! President Reagan's inauguration commenced his four-year term as President and George H. W. Bush as Vice President. The oath of office was administered by Chief Justice Warren E. Burger.

There was little President Reagan could do as far as the Rhodesian-Zimbabwe debacle, but he was able to help re-install President Somoza's position in Nicaragua, and even oust the small Communist regime that Jimmy Carter had permitted to creep into Grenada in the Caribbean. And, Mr. Reagan was instrumental in persuading the Russians (President Gorbachev) into tearing down the Berlin Wall, among many other solid accomplishments!

Also, if we remember correctly, Colonel Oliver North was detailed by Reagan to by-pass Congress, and covertly, sell arms to Iran which was engaged in a small war with Iraq at the time, so as to raise money for Nicaragua's Mr. Somoza to buy arms. As we remember, *this act was in violation of a rule that Congress had just passed that forbade any sale of arms, and so, Colonel North was charged for that under-cover operation, but was found not guilty, and remains an American hero!*

There was one instance when the terrorist group (Hezbollah) in Lebanon took over our embassy in Beirut and held our people hostage during the middle 1980's. Supposedly, our hostages were captured but held in places unknown to us! President Reagan was frustrated but couldn't attempt a rescue. Eventually, the hostages (including Terry Anderson, the head man) were freed, but the real details are a little sketchy.

An especially interesting story is this one: While watching William Buckley's PBS - *Firing Line*, in the early 1990's, the subject was the Embassy hostage situation in Lebanon. Of course, like everyone, President Ronald Reagan knew that the terrorist group, Hezbollah, had captured our people, but not the location where they were being held captive!

Mr. Buckley's guest that particular night was a distinguished white-haired British gentleman. I can't recall his name, but his story was fascinating, as revealed here. He was the retired head of the British Intelligence Service and as he told Mr. Buckley, *that,* "not too long after the U.S. Embassy people were taken hostage, the Hezbollah terrorists got a little arrogant and also captured four Russian KGB agents"! *Similarly, the Russians knew, too, that*

Hezbollah had taken their KGB men, but not where they were being held!

However, the Russians handled the situation differently, and much more effectively! The other Russian agents knew the Hezbollah group officials, and easily captured a second level Hezbollah official and then, simply castrated him! They then enclosed his genitals in a brown paper grocery bag along with a note, *"If our men are not released within 24 hours safely, this will happen to you"!* The bag was deposited on the door step of the next higher level Hezbollah official! *The official and Hezbollah got the message!* Four hours later, the four KGB men were released and were back on the street*!*

(After all, what would a gentlemanly Muslim terrorist do in Paradise, with 30 virgins, and no balls)?

This story, which the retired head of the British Intelligence Service related, is part of the many stories and facts that are told on Google, but strangely, were never in the forefront of major news stories.

(Reagan was re-elected for a second term, and his successes and exploits are well-known and no further words are needed concerning him, except to say, *Thank you*!)

President George H. Bush

George H. Bush was, as he should have been, the natural successor to Ronald Reagan. As Vice President to Ronald Reagan, he should have had no opposition to his bid for President. Before we proceed with this line of thought, let's take a look at the history of George H.

In the very early 1960's, while I was still living in Meridian, Miss., I was asked by my friend, H. W. Dailey (record producer in Houston), to appear in Houston for a fundraiser for George H. Bush. He was running for a seat in Congress, his first effort. The show was held in the Houston City Auditorium and there were a variety of acts on the show.

I remember an actress (Martha Hyer) was on the show. She walked like a "high-bred filly" and was a hard woman to forget. The show's promoters had put all of us up at the prestigious Shamrock Hotel in South Houston and I was thinking that Martha might be interested in a cup of coffee with a *"Country Boy"* and if things worked out, a little "heavy courtin'" at the hotel! But that smart classy woman, actress Martha Hyer, just up and got lost in a hurry!

I don't remember whether George H. won his seat in Congress. I do remember when he was competing for the Republican presidential nomination for President in 1980 against Ronald Reagan. And it was the opinion of a lot of folks, and still is, that Reagan really never warmed up to George H. Bush.

During the first primary debate, held in New Hampshire, there was a candidate named John Anderson from Illinois, who George H., for some reason, didn't want to be included. I remember Mr. Reagan slamming his fists down on the debate table and saying, *"I paid for this debate and he is going to be part of it"*! Of course, Ronald Reagan won the nomination and Reagan was surely urged by the Republican Party to accept George H. Bush as his Vice Presidential pick!

As, everyone expected, at the end of Reagan's two terms, George H. Bush was the next Republican nominee in 1988, and, some say, rode into victory, on Reagan's coat tails! During the next four years, Bush's big move or venture as President (presumably at the behest of Saudi Arabia in order to protect Kuwait), was the major invasion of Iraq by the United States! That invasion is known as the *Gulf Storm War*. In the years since, history shows that this might not have been the best move by Mr. Bush. However, looking back, it is always the case that if America enters into such a conflict, Americans do support their President!

A former advisor to Ronald Reagan, Patrick Buchanan did support President Bush as an American, but openly opposed the Gulf Storm War (The Invasion of Iraq.)

In 1992, President George H. Bush ran for re-election and was opposed by Patrick Buchanan. Surprisingly, Pat Buchanan almost won the first primary in New Hampshire. With such a strong showing by Buchanan, it certainly looked as though the Republican Party and its chosen candidate, George H. Bush, were going to have some rough roads ahead! I'm writing this from memory and recollections, and *I recall that Pat Buchanan and George H. Bush went on to the primary in Arizona, but some peculiar or funny things happened and somehow, George Bush ended up as the winner. Even John McCain had congratulated Buchanan on his win!*

Also, from memory, we recall that the Republican Party was concerned that Pat Buchanan might just capture the upcoming South Carolina primary, and sent Bill Bennett, a well-known Washington attorney, and Lamar Alexander,

Governor of Tennessee, to South Carolina, to urge Ralph Reed, the head of the Christian Coalition, to support George H. Bush!

At the same time, Mr. Bennett and Mr. Alexander went on to California to cultivate all the Republican precincts and officials and bring them in behind Bush.

Following this maneuvering and back stabbing (as we remember,) Pat Buchanan was rightfully infuriated, and almost resigned from the Republican Party. This brings us to these thoughts!

Patrick Buchanan opposed the George H. Bush Gulf Storm War invasion of Iraq, and Mr. Buchanan didn't like the intervention or, let's say, the meddling in the Mideast. *And, too, years later, Buchanan opposed George W. Bush's invasion of Iraq!*

So, with the election of Patrick Buchanan, rather than George H. Bush as President, the United States would not have entered into Middle Eastern affairs with the ramifications that have followed through the years, including the George W. Bush years! Something to think about!

In the last year or so of the George H. Bush administration, there was "Ruby Ridge", an incident in Idaho, where a so-called Right Wing extremist was set up by the FBI or ATF, and by request - unknowingly from a ATF man - altered the barrel of a shotgun to an illegal short length which led to a covert attack by the *ATF and the FBI* on the man's home! (*This will be discussed further in the chapter of President Bill Clinton*)

(We also remember that George H. Bush, with a United Nations mandate, sent Marines and an American force into Somalia to settle and relieve those citizens from being brutally mistreated towards the end of his administration. More on this in the Bill Clinton story)!

Yet, George H. Bush did honestly have the best interests of our country in his heart and even with his *Read My Lips* lie, falls short of being a candidate for membership of the *Washington Weasels Association*!

President Bill Clinton

(Star Member of the Washington Weasels Association)

Breaker 19, Breaker, Breaker, 19, Come on!

Yeah, I hear you there, Breaker, you got the ol' Pill Pusher here, come on!

Yeah, appreciate it, Pill Pusher, readin' you loud and clear, you got the Tuscaloosa Tom Cat here. We're headin' west on this ol' Interstate 30, out to California way. We gonna drop a load at Shaky Town and go on up to Gay City and take on a load, and head back home again!

Anyhow, ya'll look out your winder and you'll see that little ol' town they still call Hope"! Yeah, they had that big happenin' some 65 or some-odd years ago, and little ol' Slick Willie popped up in this ol' world, just a-kickin' and a-squallin'!

Yeah, I hear you there, Tom Cat, things ain't been the same since, huh?

Ten Four there, Pill Pusher! I'm signin' off here. We'll catch you later! Pedal to the Metal, ya'll, clear back to Little Rock!

The above is a fictitious version of similar conversations between truck drivers that we just might (and sometimes do) hear when we're driving that stretch of 'ol Interstate 30, passing on the outskirts of Hope, Arkansas!

No doubt about it, *ol' Slick Willie* is a likeable guy! It's hard to write disparagingly about someone that we want to like, and it's hard not to like Bill Clinton! But, that in no way means that we want him back in the White House, or anywhere in the vicinity! *Nor his wife, Hillary!*

On a personal note, I suppose that to try and find a comparable and similar couple to Bill and Hillary, we would probably have to go back in time to the late 1800's to the Old Wild West and look up Frank James, (outlaw leader of the James Gang) with his outlaw partner and lady, Belle Starr, who was, according to history, one hell of a woman, and a dead shot with a pistol. Now, at this point, let's remind ourselves not to add too much glamour to these two couples, *(Frank and Belle, and Bill and Hillary!)*

There was never much said or written about *Frank and Belle*, in the way of deceit or lying. They were just outlaws and simply held up stagecoaches and robbed trains and banks. As we know, that ain't the case with Bill and Hillary! Think in terms of them, husband and wife, as world class "fibbers", both being lawyers with a law firm in Little Rock, Arkansas, with at least Bill possessing the most essential endearment factors of *likeability and personality. Absolutely, the two most important factors needed for involvement with the public!* Or, more especially, politics, such as serving as Governor of Arkansas, and later as President of the United States!

We're all pretty well familiar with Bill Clinton's record and actions as president, and with Hillary's record and actions as first Lady; and too, let's not forget her debacle as Secretary of State under Barack Obama!

And so, to emphasize, what was true over a hundred years ago, with outlaws Frank James and Belle Starr, is still true today with Bill and Hillary Clinton! *Tolerate 'em if possible, pray for 'em, but don't trust 'em!*

As we've remarked throughout this book, that one valuable asset, the *Endearment Factor, i*s a personality complex that somehow eludes most big-wigs of the Eastern segment of the Republican Party! These folks, including the Bushes, McCains, Romneys, Cornyns, etc., all seem to have undergone major surgery for *charisma bypasses*! Whether a person is an entertainer or a politician, *without charisma or an endearment factor* it's extremely hard to be elected to office, and almost impossible to be a real success in show business!

Just the mention of Johnny Cash, Jerry Lee Lewis, Frank Sinatra, Elvis Presley, Dean Martin, etc., and we're talking about entertainers with *personality and endearment factors! Such factors are an absolute must for entertainers and singers. And for successful long-time politicians! The time frame of success for those without it is very limited!*

We might mention, for example, one very fine talent, Charlie Rich, a fine singer and musician-piano player. I happened to be booked and working at the Golden Nugget Casino in Las Vegas, when at the height of Charlie's career, with his RCA million seller, *Behind Closed Doors*, the Hilton Hotel in Las Vegas brought in Charlie to headline for a month. Charlie's show drew well, but overall, was pretty dry! (And, some of the folks in the audience were plainly *snoring too loud)*! So, the Hilton was forced to build and create a show that would move with energy around Charlie, and help to invigorate the audience. That doesn't mean that Charlie wasn't a fine musician or singer; he just wasn't an entertainer. I knew Charlie casually and liked him; he just lacked the essential ingredient: the *endearment factor.*

On the other hand, Liberace was not only a piano player, but a *captivating entertainer who was* blessed w*ith a tremendous endearment factor! But, a question:* Could the Republican Party engage the entertainment department of a Las Vegas hotel, let's say, to create and build some sort of an aura and endearment factor around a Mitt Romney, John McCain, Cornyn, or Bush? Create, for instance, a *charismatic, endearing makeover, including common sense, for Mitt Romney?*

Well, for Romney, McCain, Cornyn, etc., two chances: *Slim and None*! There would be a slim possibility, for campaign appearances only, with a mainly rehearsed speech, a top band and show to please and warm up the crowd and, importantly, to provide musical bumps during the candidate's speech! Plus, a great emcee and an award-winning introduction! *But for campaign appearances only!*

For debates, where the candidate is dependent on his or her own personality, it would be a little more difficult. Try to remember McCain and Romney's 2008 and 2012 campaigns. *And then, forget both of them and their campaigns as fast as possible!*

Actually, now that we can think about this situation, and without changing any of the above writings, we might expand on the subject somewhat, with the thoughts that with the proper group, and show, etc., the complete and total appearance and speech of the candidate could be embellished, tailored and produced to almost perfection!

Back to Las Vegas, it was interesting to note that in 1967 or 1968, after making no personal appearances for a period of about seven years, (Elvis had only been seen starring in movies), Elvis Presley's manager, Tom Parker, brought Elvis back into the public with a full schedule of personal appearances, beginning with a four week stand at that same Hilton Hotel in Las Vegas! Needless to say, people from around the world packed the Hilton for all of his engagements week after week.

We might also say that there were two entertainers, who, when they were playing Las Vegas, not only filled the hotel where they were performing, but literally filled every hotel in Vegas during the days or weeks they were performing. We are speaking of both Elvis and Frank Sinatra.

Let's repeat once again: o*l' Slick Willie* is a likeable guy! He had no problem overcoming George H. Bush's campaign and becoming our President.

Just a few months after Bill Clinton assumed the presidency, one of Bill and Hillary's closest associates, Vince Foster, (with the relationship going back to their law firm in Little Rock and holding the position of counsel to the President with his office in the White House), suddenly and apparently, committed suicide. This story has very muddy details.

Mr. Foster, leaving his office in the afternoon, had informed his secretary that he would be right back. Some hours later, they found him shot to death in his car in Fort Marcy Park, a suburb of D.C. Various thoughts floated around, with some thinking that he had actually been murdered, while others, along with the official ruling of death, termed it suicide. Personally, like most people, I would not want to believe that Bill or Hillary had anything to do with Mr. Foster's death.

(I would suggest that interested folks go online to Google and read the extensive opinions and stories regarding this subject.)

As we mentioned earlier, President Jimmy Carter issued a blanket pardon for all Vietnam era draft dodgers so those who had moved to Canada, were free to return to the U.S. at their desire. Bill Clinton was a draft evader, in the sense, that although he had received several notices to report to the draft board for induction, which he had ignored, there were no warrant or arrest notices in effect issued for him.

In the first months of his presidency, President Clinton, and also Hillary, seemed to have a very evident dislike for the military, which possibly was natural and plausible! Saluting seemed to be maybe a little awkward. And, if I am correct, Clinton in his early months when boarding Air Force One, or the White House helicopter, ignored and wouldn't return the obligatory salutes. After a while, he grew into the presidency and the routine became more comfortable.

It was very evident that Clinton was reluctant to use our military in order to show strength. That great quote, *An Ounce of Prevention* remains good advice for the U.S.! Use our great military, not to meddle in the governments of other countries such as Egypt, Libya, or the Ukraine, etc., but to teach other countries not to meddle in ours!

Looking back, for example, it appears that the first preparations of terrorist activities and attacks in the U. S. were birthed in the first years of the Clinton administration, and grew, as little effort or no serious retaliation was done to prevent such oncoming acts.

The World Trade Center bombing incident occurred early on, in the first couple of months (February 26, 1993) into the Clinton presidency, with huge destruction, 6 killed and many injured!

Our embassies in Kenya and Tanzania were also destroyed with impunity, leaving hundreds dead and injured. I believe that it was about this time that President Clinton ordered a number of cruise missiles to be fired over into Sudan (one of the Middle Eastern countries), resulting in the destruction of a pharmaceutical pill factory! A sort of: *Let's just shoot over there amongst 'em, and maybe some of us will have some relief!* Also, there was the sad debacle of Black Hawk down in Somalia, but we find no fault with Clinton's actions in that situation.

Then, came the *USS Cole*. On or about October 12, 2000, while anchored in the harbor in Yemen, a suicide boat with explosives was attached by Al Qaida to one of our latest and most advanced destroyers, the *USS Cole*, and heavily damaged it, killing 17 of our sailors. This happened in the latter months of the Clinton administration, and is a part of the pattern of Al Qaida setting up and strengthening their presence in the U.S. The terrorists involved in the 9-11 debacle had already arrived in the U.S. several years before the George W. Bush Administration, and had been taking flying lessons in order to perpetuate the attack and fly the airliners into the Twin Towers!

Interestingly, sometime before, our CIA had located the hideout of Osama bin Laden (in Afghanistan) and requested permission of President Clinton to bomb the bin Laden site with missiles from our warships steaming off the coast of Pakistan. The President O.K.'d the strike, however, his Secretary of State, Ms. Madeline Albright - a courteous lady - naively picked up the telephone, and notified the Pakistani intelligence that, "Our Navy would shortly be firing missiles over Pakistan into Afghanistan in order to destroy bin Laden", who our CIA had under surveillance!

As soon as Ms. Albright hung up the phone, the Pakistanis picked up the phone and informed Osama Bin Laden to *get your ass on your came and hit the road, the Americans are about to bomb the hell out of both your ass, and your camel!* As a result, no harm was inflicted on bin Laden! Oh, well, as we said, Ms. Albright was a courteous lady with good intentions!

(The ABC Network, I believe, produced and aired an excellent two or three hour movie of the above incident, which many of you will recall.)

Not too long ago, in approximately early August 2014, after the above writing, but prior to the publishing of this book, Bill Clinton admitted that he could have gotten bin Laden at this particular time, but he would have been firing missiles into a populated area, and so, he didn't! An interesting admission that is not too far from what we think is the truthful, above version with Ms. Albright.

As we wrote earlier, in the final year or so of the George H. Bush presidency, there was *Ruby Ridge*, the incident in Idaho, where a so-called "Right Wing" extremist was set up by the FBI or ATF, and by request - unknowingly, from an ATF man - altered the barrel of a shotgun to an illegal short length which then, led to a covert attack by the "ATF and FBI" on the man's home, and the killing of the man's 14 year-old son being shot in the back, and the man's wife being killed by an FBI sniper, while standing in their front door holding her baby!

No FBI or ATF man was charged with murder by the federal government, however, as I remember, the state of Idaho did file charges and the Feds did pay about one plus million dollars to the man's family.

The Mt. Carmel debacle near Waco, Texas, with the compound surrounded by military and the National Guard, ended a 51-day standoff which culminated in 81 deaths! This stand-off was an attempted surprise arrest on the leader, David Koresh, who evidently had no knowledge that any authorities were even interested in trying to arrest him. He had been in Waco the day before and chatted with the Sheriff but woke up the next morning to find soldiers, military equipment, and even tanks surrounding the compound!

The onslaught was evidently set off when tear gas grenades were fired by the order of Janet Reno, Attorney General for President Clinton. The tear gas grenades set off a fire and turned the entire compound into an inferno, resulting in the deaths of all 81 people inside! No government official was ever charged!

Ruby Ridge, of course, had no connection to the Mount Carmel debacle near Waco, Texas, except that both incidents which involved the ATF and FBI further enraged a right wing extremist, Timothy McVey, to the point that he caused, and was responsible for, the disastrous bombing of the Federal Building in Oklahoma City. This subject has been so thoroughly written about that there is no need to go further!

No doubt about it, Bill Clinton was re-elected to a second term, not so much as having had a successful administration, but simply because he is a likeable man! He was actually impeached during the latter part of his final term because of his lying under oath: *I never had sex with that woman*, referring to Monica Lewinsky. But, it was never about the *act of sex, but about the act of lying!* Due to his having only a few months left to serve in his term, and voted not guilty by the Senate, it was decided that Bill should serve out the remaining time, as President!

(Also, in approximately the mid- summer of 2014, Hillary Clinton confided to ABC's Diane Sawyer that she and her husband, Bill Clinton, were dead broke when he left the presidency. As of now, December 2014, with Hillary receiving a $14,000,000 advance on her book, their net worth is about $55,000,000. Hardly broke!

Sarah Palin

Speaking again of that all-important *endearment factor*, we are reminded that Texas has been blessed with Republicans who do have personality, such as Governor Rick Perry, or Senator Ted Cruz; and, there are some others, although not Texans, such as Rick Santorum and Marco Rubio, who are blessed with the *endearment factor*. And, let's not forget that Newt Gingrich and Dick Cheney are likeable! Of course, we will never forget one of our favorite ladies, the former governor of Alaska, Sarah Palin, the best part of the McCain/Palin duo!

By the way, some of Rush Limbaugh's *Lower Information Voters* and certain liberal Democratic politicians tended to make light of Sarah Palin. A word of advice and caution to those folks! As Merle Haggard would sing, *When you're runnin' down our Sarah, man, you're walkin' on the fightin' side of me"!*

It's a damned shame, too, that certain journalists and reporters, especially those with NBC, such as Chuck Todd and Peter Alexander - although they know better - are willing to let stand (without correction), the episode on *Saturday Night Live* where Tina Fey, (playing the part of Sarah Palin) jokes, *and I can see Russia from my backyard!* Of course, without correction, this leaves some average viewers with the impression that Sarah Palin herself actually made the statement! (This happened on Chuck Todd's *Meet The Press* January 4-2015). Pretty shabby actions from Chuck and Peter. Several folks who sent e-mails said that apologies and some good *ass-kickings* are in order!

It's certainly no surprise that ol' Chuck and Peter are involuntarily voted Star Members of the Washington Weasels Association!

Senator Kirsten Gillibrand

While we're on the subject of sex in Washington, we are reminded that members of Congress are poor examples of fidelity. Now, to tell the truth, almost all of us, but especially members of Congress, have all been *over the hill, around the bend, across the creek, and treed a 'coon or two! But, most members of Congress are outstanding in this field!*

Currently, as of this writing, and this is important, Ladies and Gentlemen, there is a storm or war of allegations of misconduct (mostly sexual misbehavior) being waged against our Military! Now, no one would try to say that our military (officers and men and women) are *squeaky clean* to the point of not enjoying the favors of the opposite sex. And, this is how it should be! *The great General Patton used to say that "a soldier who won't f***, won't fight"!* And, a part of that comment is probably true! But, dangerously, there is without doubt, a calculated movement among the Obama Administration (and some members of Congress), to demean, weaken and lower our Armed Forces to the point of neither being able to prevent, or conduct, a *major war-like exercise if needed.* Far too many generals, admirals, and high level officers have been forced into retirement by Obama. *And these are troubled times!*

Now, here is the point! There seems to be a plethora of charges against our military, charges of lying and cheating on exams, for example, by some who are responsible for manning our nuclear deterrent facilities, but more so, charges of sexual molestation. No charges of rape, but for the most part, pertaining to unwanted advances. Whatever that means! Always, in the past, our military has satisfactorily handled such problems within the military. But …

There is a newly elected Democratic Senator, Ms. Kirsten Gillibrand, working with a zeal, to remove the military's option to handle problems such as sex molestation, etc., and place those problems in the hands of Congress! Now, folks, how many members of Congress could be trusted to better assume those duties than our military? I mean, what the hell, former Congressman Barney Frank's live-in companion in Washington, D. C. actually operated a "whore house", aka call service, for prostitutes whether male or female, or both, out of Barney's home in Washington for several years without his knowledge! *Or so he says!*

As most knowledgeable and thinking people believe, the remaining vestiges of Honor are in our military and police departments, and most definitely, not in Congress! Can we visualize a committee of Congressmen composed of members with the morals and integrity of Barney Frank, Anthony Weiner, and, yes, headed up by Senator Hillenbrand, judging our men and women in uniform? (For extra integrity, we could always add Senators Dick Durban, Chuck Schumer, Harry Reid, and Congresswomen Nancy Pelosi, and from Houston, Sheila Jackson).

That being said, we should emphasize again to Senator Hillenbrand that honor does not reside in members of Congress, but in our military. And, stop meddling!

TheMujahedeen-Taliban-Osama-Bin Laden
(with the late Congressman, Charlie Wilson)

To further show and emphasize that our country, by meddling in the affairs of other countries in which we have no business, consider the following: In the 1980's there were serious developments and movements underway in Afghanistan. And this writing and interpretation of those happenings underscore just how easily our country, by *messing around* in the affairs of other countries, can slide into and become a factor in those affairs, mostly to our detriment!

We remember that for a period of about seven years, Russia was involved in a war in Afghanistan, *strangely, not against the Afghan government, but actually by its invitation,* to help fight against a terrorist group, called the Mujahedeen. That same group, - the Mujahedeen - is now called the Taliban!

There was a fairly prominent Democratic U.S. Congressman (the late Charlie Wilson) from Lufkin, Texas, who somehow managed to finagle our government to begin furnishing weapons and arms (especially Stinger missiles) along with billions in American cash, to the Mujahedeen! Congressman Wilson even went to Afghanistan and lived with the Mujahedeen, for a short time.

Now here is the interesting part. With a contingent of foreign Afghan-Arabs who were involved and working with the Mujahedeen (helped by Charlie Wilson) in Afghanistan, there was a **younger Osama bin Laden!** This *Afghan-Arab group of bin Ladens,* eventually became **Al Qaida!** And as we know, Russia eventually called it quits, packed up, and pulled out of Afghanistan. Now, the question: was our *meddling* - the billions in American taxpayer cash and weapons to the *("Mujahedeen" -"Taliban")* - worth the effort?

Well, we found out on 9-11! We also might mention that recently our government announced that the Afghan government would henceforth be fighting the Taliban terrorists (the former Mujahedeen) on its own without US help.

So, after thousands of U.S. soldiers losing their lives and billions of dollars spent, it would appear *as though we're right back to the exact same situation as we were in 1998!*

Hillary Clinton

(The following is Hillary Clinton being interviewed, I believe, with Joe Schoffstall of Capital City Projects. We would all expect that a potential presidential candidate (such as Hillary Clinton) during a filmed interview, would certainly be able to present a logical, cogent, and proud response as to her accomplishments as Secretary of State! Well, maybe not! Hillary's actual response:

"My accomplishments as Secretary of State? Well, I'm glad you asked! My proudest accomplishment in which I take the most pride, mostly because of the opposition it faced early on, you know… the remnants of prior situations and mindsets that were too narrowly focused in a manner whereby they may have overlooked the bigger picture and we didn't do that and I'm proud of that. Very proud! I would say that's a major accomplishment."

Do you get it, folks? Hillary's clear, logical, answers?

Actually, some of the most detrimental actions that Hillary was a part of *(with verbal support from John McCain and zero protest from Senator John Cornyn)* was to help Obama orchestrate a prolonged bombardment of Egypt, and Libya, which destroyed the governments, rulers, and internal structure of those countries. This helped set the stage for the present turmoil and over-all devastation that we are now involved in, and currently witnessing in the Mideast! It still continues!

Egypt had been, since the days of Jimmy Carter, the primary peace buffer between Israel and the Palestinians! Thanks to Hillary and Obama, that peace buffer (put in place by Egyptian President Anwar Sadat, and the Prime Minister of Israel, and sponsored by President Jimmy Carter), is sadly, *totally and senselessly lost!*

Prior to Hillary Clinton being named to be Obama's Secretary of State, many of us had thoughts that she would probably be hugely successful in that position in establishing firmer and more cordial relations with almost all foreign countries, especially those countries which were already allies or border-line friendly to the U.S. After all, she had been a *world traveler as First Lady in the White House for*

8 years with Bill Clinton, and should have already been familiar, respected, and on a first name basis with many of the world's leaders.

However, that turned out to be wishful thinking, with the majority of the foreign leaders regarding her as best described by the president of North Korea, as, *"nothing more than a school girl flouncing around in a yellow jump suit"!* Then, as Secretary of State, she joined and helped Obama in the debacle of Egypt and Libya, and then came the lies, excuses, and attempted cover-up of the Benghazi incident. As a result of this and other involvements by Ms. Clinton, she has actually zero credibility.

Now, this would be a good opportunity to measure Hillary Clinton in comparison with another former Secretary of State under George W. Bush, Condoleezza Rice. We all remember Condoleezza as impeccably dressed and well-groomed, with an always calm and a business-like manner. Also, her appearance and good looks invited admiration and respect from many of the world leaders, of whom several became enamored with her.

The late and former ruler of Libya, (Muammar Khadafy) was said to have been so hung up on Condoleezza that he kept an autographed photo of her on his desk.

Speaking of Hillary's credibility, we may recall an incident several years ago during the uprising and rebellion in the Balkans, when Ms. Clinton was on a fact-finding, plus good-will, mission. As her plane was landing, they - in the words of Ms. Clinton - "came under sniper fire." Well, that turned out to be one of the "whoppers" that both she and her husband Bill, are notorious for! There was *no sniper fire*, but there *was* a nice luncheon buffet spread waiting for her and her party at the airport!

Strange how Hillary mistook a table loaded with good vittles such as, filet mignon, sliced melon, and Chablis, for sniper- fire.

Still, she retains that certain core of people, liberals and today's Democrats, who appear to wear blinders. Whether this loyal moronic following is large enough to support her and the Democratic Party's efforts to assure her the Democratic nomination for President in 2016, will be interesting!

We can know why some of the ladies in the Democratic Party, such as Nancy Pelosi and Sheila Jackson, blindly follow! These are women who are into environmental issues and know all about the Spotted Owl, but otherwise, as one comedian said, are so *dumb* they think a woodpecker is a decoy!

What we do remember is Hillary's comment and answer when she was testifying to a Congressional committee concerning her involvement (as Secretary of State) in the Benghazi incident in Libya, where four members of our Embassy staff, plus our Ambassador was killed, Hillary's response was: *What difference does it make?*

Both President Bill Clinton and Hillary each remain star members of The Washington Weasels Association.

Vice President Al Gore

Star Member of The Washington Weasels Association

An Inconvenient Truth

Well, *global warming* is back in the forefront of our news with Al Gore leading the pack! Probably not many of us remember or know just when the *global warming* topic (truth or theory) began. One puzzle unanswered to many folks, Democrats and Republicans, is; *How did Al Gore become involved and how did he make (or earn) One Hundred Million Dollars in only a year or so?*

The answer, I believe, is contained in some articles published in *Time Magazine* during the summer months of 2009-2011. One of the most telling articles was written by Michael Scherer, who is a very solid writer. Here's my gist of the story:

During the last few months of the Clinton Administration, a man named John Doerr, who was a mover and shaker in Silicon Valley and had raised some millions for corporations such as Hewlett-Packard, came to Washington D.C. with an idea and a brand new corporation named Kleiner-Berg. As a multi-millionaire and a big contributor to the Democratic Party - almost like "home folks" - he easily managed to get into the office of then Vice President Al Gore. *The Plan* was to raise both government participation and financing for Kleiner-Berg. The government would put some millions in grants behind *The Plan,* and as soon as was feasible, the government would put *The Plan* into operation. Specifically, *The Plan* was a program for lower income people wherein their homes and buildings would be updated with new siding and insulation, thus bringing them up to government standards.

Gore took John Doerr and *The Plan* into the office of President Clinton who immediately loved the program and approved $500 Million dollars for Kleiner-Berg. In approximately 2006, Gore had helped with and had narrated the documentary, *An Inconvenient Truth,* and somehow, he was made a partner in Kleiner-Berg.

Since the Clinton Administration was leaving, to be replaced by George Bush, the Kleiner-Berg program lay dormant through the Bush years during which the global warming, and *Inconvenient Truth* documentaries, etc., advanced the promotion of *The Plan*! Shortly after Obama took office, *The Plan* or *Program* was put into effect.

Did Gore sell or use his office to acquire the partnership in Kleiner-Berg? Was President Clinton a beneficiary? Do bears live in the woods? Just thought you'd like to know!)

World Climate Change
(And Deep Thoughts)!

Is climate change (fact or theory) caused by man-made pollution or by naturally occurring phenomena happening throughout the centuries? It makes us wonder. What about the great volcanic explosion of Krakatoa in 1883, the most destructive volcanic explosion in history, when the smoke, fog, and pollution covered and filled the world's oceans and atmosphere for many months? How did that affect the overall climate, and for how long? All the man-made pollution for periods of years could not even begin to equal that one time, cataclysmic event!

One of the television network's morning news shows (CBS), frequently features an Oriental gentleman with long white hair, Michio Kaku (a nice little man), and I believe, a scientist and Harvard professor, who espouses the global warming theory. He has no doubts as to the truth of his belief, *The Earth is heating up!* A likeable person, he is also symbolic of the global warming crowd who just won't tolerate or even consider, opposing views!

Interestingly enough, some 40-odd years ago, I became a fan, or adherent, of the late and great Russian scientist, Immanuel Vilokovsky, who has been disavowed and derided by most of the scientific community because of his unusual theories and writings.

For example (and this is one of Vilokovsky's beliefs), every 7,000 - 10,000 years, the ice builds up on one of the earth's polar caps to the extent that *the Planet, due to the extreme weight of the billions of tons of ice on the Polar Zone Cap, and gravitational impulses,* actually becomes topsy-turvy, and eventually flip-flops, causing the Polar Cap to become an equatorial zone. And, the then equatorial zone naturally attains a new position, and becomes the new Polar Cap (or Zone).

If this sounds like fantasy, consider: *In Siberia, (Our North Polar Cap) prehistoric animals, such as crocodiles, mammoths, etc., are still buried in the ice and through the years, have been eaten by the natives, causing us to wonder how those animals which are of equatorial origin and habitat, perished, and were frozen so swiftly, that their flesh is still safely eaten!* Also, according to Vilikovský, there are (were) hand drawn maps in a Turkish embassy, which show the South Pole not only to be free of ice and snow, but with forests of trees and plants!

Also, interestingly, the huge Lake Victoria in Africa was once a Polar Cap with its waters, resulting from the melting of that Polar Ice Cap.

Over 4,000 years ago, during the biblical times of Abraham, Isaac, and Jacob, the prevailing winds blowing over Africa blew the moisture and rains from Lake Victoria over Egypt, causing the rains and prosperity, while the other areas were suffering an extreme drought!

The Bible reveals that Joseph, son of Jacob, was sold into the captivity of a caravan on its way to Egypt, and while there, he became a favorite of the Pharaoh. He later brought his relatives including his father, Jacob, and the family over into Egypt to live and enjoy the crops and prosperity there due to the rains and moisture being blown over Egypt from Lake Victoria! As we read, they remained for many years (about 400 I believe), until Moses led them out of Egypt into the *Promised Land!*

The area of the Great Salt Lake flats, Death Valley, and down through the Salton Sea area in

California was once a Polar Cap, with the great weight of the ice depressing the earth to below sea level.

Oh, well, so much for Global Warming!

As an item of interest (a story I related in my autobiography), some very fine people, devout environmentalists, Ted Turner and his actress and former wife, Jane Fonda, are caught up and dedicated totally to preserving the environment.

Several years ago, while in Billings, Montana, for a few days, I remember a rumor that Ted and Jane, still living on their ranch at the time in Montana, were so *caught up* in the idea of conserving water that they would undergo several dumps before flushing the commode! That story could have been only a rumor, but if true, a *good outhouse* would have solved that dilemma, and maybe prevented a divorce!

Like most folks, not knowing them personally, I like Ted and Jane, and think they are good Americans, even with her messing around in Vietnam! Recently, we've all seen Jane stripped down in her exercise gym suit ads, and she's still a *Purty good lookin' woman!*

The Utah State Bird

Speaking earlier of the Great Salt Flats - and this is in no way related to climate change - in or around the 1850's, people of the Mormon faith had settled and populated the state of Utah. The hard working Mormons were prosperous with great farms and ranches, but suddenly, massive hordes of locusts, numbering in the millions, moved in across the state and began devouring the crops and stripping all vegetation! Having no protection against the locusts, the Mormons prayed and appealed to a higher power, God! As if in answer, flocks and flocks of California Seagulls began to arrive over Utah and consumed the entire influx of locusts! The ranches, pastures, and crops were saved! And so, the

Utah State legislature gratefully voted the *Seagull* as the *Utah State Bird!*

The Earth's Inner Core (Fictional Pellucidar)

While on the subject of world climate change and being showered by the probable "fairy-tales" of the global warming crowd, it's interesting to note that scientists have recently revealed that a *vast pool* or *Sea of Water* has been discovered in the interior of our Planet Earth! This ocean is larger and contains more water than all of the top-side or surface oceans combined. Truly, something to even think about!

This brings to mind that the renowned author, the late Edgar Rice Burroughs, was blessed with one of the most fantastic imaginations that have ever been known. While having written the entire catalog of Tarzan novels, Mr. Burroughs also created an entire civilization on the planet Mars, complete with tribes, nations, governments, etc., with those many novels called the *Martian* series.

But he also wrote and created a series of novels about our *Earth's Inner Core*, a world called

Pellucidar, in which he detailed the travels and adventures of the fictionalized student, Jason Gridley, who, with his teacher, *the elder Professor Perry,* entered into the center of the Earth through an opening near the North Pole! Descending into the Earth for many, many miles, they eventually came to the Earth's core, and found a vast ocean and civilization complete with a *Sun that never set, and a world of tribes, nations, and animals.* The peoples and animals were, of course, of a pre-historic appearance with a culture of a war-like nature, except that the women were all prone to be beautiful.

Naturally, our hero, Jason Gridley, ended up marrying a princess and eventually returned with her to the Earth's surface for a time before returning to live in their Kingdom below in *Pellucidar*!

In keeping with the mind and imagination of the late Edgar Rice Burroughs, this particular series of novels is a great read.

And, without questioning the truth of our scientists' new discovery of the huge oceans lying beneath our earth's surface, those discovering scientists might think about and consider a similar Jason Gridley type exploration. Something to think about!

President George W. Bush

From an average citizen's view and opinion, President George W. Bush was not one of our great presidents, but with the huge problem of 9-11 occurring shortly after his election, he was faced with immediate emergencies that demanded some decisions which many of our presidents, thankfully, have not had to face.

Certainly, we had to go after the bin Laden group who were in Afghanistan! However, whether or not we should have invaded Iraq is another matter. In retrospect, and in view of the billions in cost, not to mention the thousands of lives that were lost, and the current and continuing problems, it would seem that most of us would agree with Patrick Buchanan, that it was not an advisable move. *Of course,* President Bush assured us that our financial cost of going into Iraq would be more than paid for from the huge oil sales of the Iraqi oil reserves ...*Sure!*

Maybe Saddam did have weapons of mass destruction which were not found, maybe it was finishing Daddy's (George H. Bush) business, and maybe as we heard, Saddam had supposedly sent someone to assassinate former President George H. Bush? As many pundits think, since Saddam Hussein and bin Laden did not like each other, quite possibly, Saddam could have greatly assisted us with eradicating bin Laden and the Al Qaida group! (At the very least, Saddam certainly had a firm grip and control of the government and functions of Iraq).

However, as good Americans, we all

supported George W. Bush as our president!

The Hurricane Katrina was another emergency that George H. did handle very well, but for some reasons, caught a lot of undeserved criticism from Democrats and the news media! It seemed to be the fact that he flew over the area in Air Force One instead of arriving in a helicopter, as he did the following day, that opened the door to the *cries* and *whines* from the *always liberal* news media, (NBC, ABC, CBS, and of course, the *"Squirrel Cage", MSNBC!* George W. offered the services of our military, but both the Louisiana Governor, and New Orleans' Mayor Ray Nagin, turned down his offers to assist.

What they didn't turn down was President Bush ordering FEMA to smother the New Orleans area *with about 80 billion dollars in federal aid.* Senator Mary Landrieu of Louisiana, not too long ago in a campaign ad, with her father sitting beside her, said that she got *billions* for Louisiana, taking credit for the billions received! *(Come on, Mary, we like you okay, but, give Bush a little credit! He had already given those billions to Louisiana)!*

Also, during the Katrina days, each resident with a driver's license registered in the New Orleans area was eligible to receive $2,000 in emergency *walking around* money, and that same driver's license could be presented in any hotel or restaurant in the United States, and FEMA would pay the bill.

In the casinos in Baton Rouge, Lake Charles, and Shreveport, the dealers at the black jack and crap tables, and in the poker rooms, openly loved and appreciated that FEMA *money being spread around*!

We remember that over 1,000 recreational vehicles (travel trailers) were purchased for emergency accommodations, and for the most part were never used, but were parked in fields about 80 miles north of New Orleans, near Hattiesburg, Miss. Through the next several years, the homes and trailers were stripped of the interiors, such as toilets, etc., by enterprising vandals! *Still*, Bush caught criticism.

Throughout this book, we've talked about that most valuable asset, the *endearment factor*. Being from Texas, George W. just naturally had a touch of that grace, and for that, we liked him. There were a few times (I thought) when as Governor of Texas he could have certainly *endeared* himself even more so with a little extra compassion.

For example, consider the lady, Carla Faye Tucker, who was in prison on death row. Sure, she had committed a heinous crime by killing a woman in a drug induced rage and was rightfully given the death penalty by a jury. However, for the several years prior to the execution date, she had been redeemed spiritually, and was well-known for doing good work among fellow inmates with compassionate care and Christianity. She had appealed for clemency and the opportunity to speak with Gov. Bush, but, quite frankly, Bush never took time to talk with the woman! He conveniently disposed of the problem by tossing the decision over into the hands of the Lord saying, *May God have mercy on her soul*! Bush's request to the Lord may have helped Carla in the afterlife, but didn't do her any good in this one!

We remember Cindy Sheehan whose soldier son was killed in Iraq. She camped outside the gate of the road which led up to Bush's ranch house in Crawford, Texas, day after day, week after week, in the hope of being able to talk with President Bush! Inevitably, anti-war protesters, the curious, and the news media began to make it a small circus event! Just for a moment, let's look at this from the mind of Ms. Sheehan.

Her son had been killed in Iraq, and she was not completely satisfied with the military's explanation and circumstances. And what we would have loved to see, instead of driving blithely on past her in his limousine, is George Bush, just once, lowering the car window, as I believe Ronald Reagan would probably have done, saying, *Come on up to the house and have some lunch, Cindy! I believe Laura's gettin' ready to put it on the table*! That small touch would have endeared George W. to millions of new fans, and added a *touch of greatness!*

As we said, George W. Bush was an adequate president and we can find no good reason for him to be inducted as a member of the *Washington Weasels Association.*

Senator John McCain, Republican, Arizona

(Member of the Washington Weasels Association)

It's not easy to write critically about a United States senator who is a Vietnam War hero and was tortured by the Viet Cong. But the fact is, that McCain, in joining Obama and Hillary Clinton in making war against, and participating in the destruction of the Egyptian government (friendly to us, and with a peace pact with Israel for 30 years), defies all common sense and is incomprehensible!

Along with the destabilization of Egypt and the Mideast, this action helped put the *Muslim Brotherhood* (which seems to be Obama's other family) into power in Egypt, if only for a short time, as even the Egyptian people couldn't stomach the *Muslim Brotherhood,* its *President Mohamed Morsi,* nor the *U.S. President Obama!* They wasted no time in tossing out Morsi and his *Brotherhood* with new elections.

However, during the brief time the Muslim Brotherhood was in control of Egypt, President Obama managed to give a billion and a half dollars of the American taxpayer's cash, plus a large amount of armaments, including jet fighters, to Mr. Morsi and the Muslim Brotherhood, which of course, as we said earlier, also owns and controls Hamas, the terrorist group, which is an avowed enemy of Israel! *(And, without any objections from McCain, Cornyn, Nancy Pelosi, Barbara Boxer, or any of the* "leaky vessel" *bunch who compose our Congress!)*

Obama's method of making war on, let's say, a country which is a small nation and unable to defend itself, is not by going to Congress to declare war, but to act by "executive authority", and cajole two or three small allies such as France or Italy, to station a couple of ships offshore and, with *Obama* (the U.S.) supplying the bombs and missiles, bomb and destroy the helpless nation until its government and leaders are killed or forced to step down!

And that's exactly what has happened in the last several years. For example, in Egypt and Libya (with the U.S. attacking and demolishing the internal structure of those two nations), such actions also helped to shred our image with almost all of the other Mideast countries! (*A clear example of seemingly, power-struck, inept amateurs temporarily caught up in euphoria, and making dangerous and incredibly foolish mistakes with long-lasting consequences!*)

Although Libya was not the ally and friend, as was Egypt, it was not, and had not been a threat since the early days of Ronald Reagan. Nevertheless, Obama's (unconfirmed) reason for the destruction of Libya and Muammar Khadafy was that Mr. Khadafy was intending to murder several thousand of his people in a small town. The end result is that Khadafy has been killed, Al-Sharia is predominant, our ambassador and several of our people have been killed, and our embassy destroyed! Libya is in turmoil, caused by the machinations of Obama and Hillary Clinton, causing even more destabilization for the Mideast, and additional breeding grounds for terrorists.

It's *an additional headache* of our own making for our country to cope with! As we know, since these writings, the situation in the Mideast has worsened with at least four other terrorist groups, such as ISIS being formed, and now, with most of the entire Mideast in turmoil, formerly friendly or neutral countries, are either antagonistic or suspicious, and don't or can't trust us! From somewhat not quite safe, but still, by comparison, peaceful situations, we are now in very perilous times.

While disapproving of, and of course, not understanding the amateurish actions of Obama, the fact that Hillary Clinton, former Secretary of State, and Senator John McCain foolishly being a part of these preposterous actions, is also in no way understandable!

We take no joy in mentioning again, that Romney, in giving McCain all of his delegate votes in the 2008 presidential primary race, enabled *McCain to beat out Mike Huckabee! However, Obama won due to McCain's flabby performance.*

And, of course, in 2012, Romney popped up again with the backing of the Republican Party, outspent all the other candidates, and naturally lost, costing the country and the Republican Party the second, or 2012, presidential race. Just recently, with the urging and backing of the Republican Party, there was a strong possibility that Romney would run again in the 2016 Presidential election, and more than likely he would have lost again, for a third presidential loss! The simple truth is, Mr. Romney lacked the *"endearment factor", and worse, didn't seem to understand its necessity or value!* Thankfully, he bowed out of a possible third run.

There are strong, substantiated rumors that former Arkansas Governor Mike Huckabee will make a presidential run and, if so, he would probably make the most formidable candidate!

We should say, that while John McCain is fond of saying that, *in the Senate*, he has *the ability to reach across the aisle,* most of us would prefer to have senators who would be more inclined to *kick ass rather than compromise!*

We are *very reluctantly* inducting Senator McCain involuntarily into *The Washington Weasels Association.*

Former Governor Mitt Romney - (Star Member of the Washington Weasels Association)

It's fairly evident that the Republican Party is more and more having trouble trying to connect with the conservative base in the country. And it's not because this base doesn't have common sense. It's that the true conservative base doesn't like the overall direction of the party. No *rock-solid, firm resolve* to win, as let's witness Romney's weak performance as the Presidential candidate in 2012! In that race of 2012, the foremost Republican candidates were Newt Gingrich and Mitt Romney.

As mentioned earlier, we remember that in the 2008 Presidential race Romney had enabled John McCain to pull ahead of Mike Huckabee by unexplainably pulling out of the race, and dumping all of his delegate votes to McCain!

Even though Huckabee won the next primary in Texas, he couldn't overcome the lead given to McCain by the gift from Romney. Of course, as we know, McCain lost to Obama!

Now, nice lady that she is, Mrs. Barbara Bush's stamp of approval on a candidate, is almost the same as a "kiss of death"! As for instance:

In the Presidential race of 2012, Newt Gingrich had won handily over Romney in the first primary races in the South. Suddenly, Barbara Bush puts her stamp of approval (endorsed) on Romney, and the millions from the Republican Party came pouring into Romney's campaign!

The *lack-luster* Romney outspent Gingrich in some states such as Iowa, as much as, 30-1, and if memory serves me right, in the State of Florida it was 60-1. In other words, Romney, in the 2012 presidential race, (with the backing of his party) runs roughshod over Gingrich and the other candidates! *The result, Romney wins the Presidential primary, but, with no endearment factor, plus his refusal to stand "head to toe" with Obama (and with the helpful impediment of Candy Crowley of CNN), he just naturally loses the race to Obama*

Due to his actions in the 2008 and 2012 presidential elections, Mitt Romney becomes a member of the *Washington Weasels Association.*

Senator John Cornyn...Republican

Senator John Cornyn is a nice, elderly, dignified gentleman who has been sitting in a very comfortable Senate seat going on just about 12 years now! Sounds great and wonderful and what is needed? Well ... what we all need, of course, is an energetic senator with "balls" and common-sense sitting in that Senate chair with the will and desire to stand up and go head-to-toe with President Obama and the *leaky vessels* in Washington (the Democratic Party). Now, I confess that I'm also guilty (or will help take the credit) with the many other voters who have helped to keep Cornyn in the Senate!

I remember when Mr. Cornyn first ran for the Texas Supreme Court, there was no problem in voting for him; and a few years later, we found no reason not to vote for him again when he ran for Attorney General! And, as we know, when a man like John Cornyn, always dignified, and dressed impeccably, makes no waves, and does a passable job in those positions where decisions are hardly ever controversial, he is most generally easily re-elected!

But, aside from Senator Cornyn's Senate record in Washington (in 20001, he ran for the U.S. Senate seat of Senator Phil Gramm that was coming up for grabs and was elected), this is something that bothered me and a lot of folks at that time, as follows:

When Gov. George W. Bush began campaigning for President in the late 1990's, the Speaking Rock Casino in El Paso, Texas had been in been operation for five years. And with Bush being governor of Texas for four of those years, Bush suddenly began opposing the Casino. In a series of four articles in *Time Magazine*, in October-November 2001) author Don Barlett exposes the truths and backgrounds of the operations of Indian owned casinos in the U.S. regarding the operations and who really gets the money, etc.

In the fourth and final article titled, *Speaking Rock Casino,* Mr. Barlett rates that casino as the finest and most efficiently operated Indian owned casino of them all. The casino, operated by the Tiqua Indian tribe, had made possible new schools, a hospital, and virtually lifted the entire tribe out of poverty with good jobs, homes and living conditions. However, politics prevailed!

Under pressure from the large Baptist voting block out of Waco, Texas, and with big money coming into the picture from Las Vegas, and other gambling operations in Louisiana, and New Mexico, (all in opposition to the *Speaking Rock Casino* in El Paso), the pressure grew! As attorney general, John Cornyn used his powers to file a suit to force the closure of the Tiqua Indians' *Speaking Rock Casino*. Together, John Cornyn along with George Bush put a vise grip on the nose of an El Paso federal judge, who finally ordered the closure. And there was money involved!

The following article might be of interest! From news sources, and in Don Barlett's final article on the Tiqua Indians' *Speaking Rock Casino* for *Time Magazine*, he alleges that $1.25 million (in $250,000. payments) went to the Republican Party in Texas in appreciation of their efforts in helping to close the *Speaking Rock Casino* in El Paso, Texas. The money supposedly came from competitive interests (the Sunland Race Track and Casino) across the state line over in New Mexico!

Having said all of this, Senator John Cornyn is an honorable man and recently, is beginning to display a long overdue "toughness" in the Senate!

(and, damn it, I like to play poker).

Senator Chuck Schumer

Star Member of the Washington Weasels Association)

Senator Chuck Schumer of New York recently made the statement *(Face the Nation 1-4-2015)* that he is opposed to the Keystone Pipeline, and even if the Republicans can get together enough votes to pass the okay to build the pipeline, he thinks he can get enough Democratic votes to uphold the absolute certainty of the Obama veto!

Schumer also says that the pipeline will provide a total of only 45 jobs compared to tens of thousands of jobs which would be affected by solar and clean energy! Now, we would like for Senator Schumer to explain just what those 45 jobs provided by the Keystone would entail and where those jobs would be! Also, recognize that virtually all the solar attempts *(in particular, Solyndra in California, which received a grant of $500 million dollars from Obama)*, have bankrupted, with no production at all!

Plus, a company located in Germany to which Obama provided *a grant of $400 million dollars* to manufacture the battery which would power the Chevy Volt car, bankrupted, never having made the first battery!

In truth, the Keystone Pipeline would provide permanent jobs from the entrance of the pipeline into the United States, all checkpoints down throughout the U.S., and the various states, into Houston, and all distribution points, and/or refineries! Plus, it would assure a steady complete supply of oil to the U.S. and in addition to our already fine supply of oil from our fracking and drilling on private lands *(Obama had nothing to do with this),* would assure our complete independence from the Mideast and the world.

Also, we would like to impress on everyone, that our current huge supplies of oil produced currently here in the U.S. have been accomplished with no help from the Obama administration, but in many cases, actually *in spite* of its objecting and hindering!

(Importantly, we might mention that in the case of wind energy, the great mover and shaker, and oil tycoon, T. Boone Pickens, installed rows and rows of the huge windmills, beginning west of Abilene, Texas, and throughout West Texas, to supply power to that part of Texas. Having owned a business in Colorado City, Texas, I'm very familiar with that country. I'm not sure what happened, but T. Boone curtailed the installation of the windmills and, I understand, canceled a billion dollar order of *additional* windmills.

I travel extensively through the Midwest where especially, in Iowa, there are a lot of windmills operating. Also, I have always thought that to the east of San Francisco, California, in the mountain areas, where the windmills are plentiful (scenic and beautiful) and also in the Midwest, the free winds would be the final answer. But no! The truth is, an available abundant supply of oil is the answer. And, now we have a plentiful supply that will last for over 150 years!

And in my humble opinion, the installation of the Keystone Pipeline and the removal of Chuck Schumer from the U.S. Senate would be a double positive bonus!

<u>President Barack Hussein Obama</u>

President of the United States from 2009-2017

Star Member of The Washington Weasels Association (History)

Now, generally speaking, hardly anyone would deny that Barack Obama is one of the more prolific prevaricators (liars) that we have ever had in the White House, and Heaven knows, we have had a bunch through the years, although few, or none, in his category! Some folks are even saying that the President lies so much, that when he and Michelle decide to go for a family outing or drive he has to get someone else to call his dogs to get into the van, because even the dogs don't believe him!

And also, something that I confess I don't know a lot about, some of the folks say that Muslims are not allowed to ride in a vehicle with animals, not knowing of course, that Obama is not a Muslim, but a Christian! At least, that's what both he and the Reverend Jeremiah,*("goddam America")* Wright claim, and the Reverend Wright has taught Obama for the last twenty-five years or so. Of course, Ole Jeremiah is in Chicago, and we're not sure where the

Obamas attend church nowadays, if at all!

The Reverend Jeremiah Wright

If Jeremiah Wright was Obama's mentor, as Obama has said, what then, were some of the *Words of Wisdom* from Reverend Wright that were so molded into Obama's mind and soul? Well, could it be Ole Jeremiah saying from the pulpit, that the U.S. had brought on Al Qaida's attacks because of the terrorism of The U.S. *"We bombed Hiroshima, we bombed Nagasaki, and we nuked far more than the thousands in New York and the Pentagon, and we never batted an eye."* And, *"They want us to sing God Bless America!"* *"No, no, no, God d— America, that's in the Bible for killing innocent people. God d— America for treating our citizens as less than human"!*

The Reverend Jeremiah Wright also is quoted as saying, (in regards to Al Qaida and the 9-11 attacks in New York City), *"We have supported state terrorism against the Palestinians and Black South Africans, and now we are indignant because the stuff we have done overseas is now brought right back to our own front yards. America's chickens are coming home to roost,"* he told his congregation.

(Well, after 20 years of being indoctrinated with such anti-American rhetoric and *bullshit,* it would be a 100 percent guarantee of Obama's mind and soul being poisoned against America by the Reverend Jeremiah Wright!)

President Obama's Origin, Background, and How did he really get into politics? (Or, has he ever done anything else)?

First of all, let's talk about Obama's obviously fraudulent Social Security Number.

In a case questioning Obama's eligibility for the 2012 presidential ballot in Georgia, evidence was introduced in court to prove that the president is using a Connecticut Social Security number (he never lived in Connecticut), that this Social Security number was never really issued to Obama, and was originally issued to another person!

Obama's lawyer, Michael Jablonski, tried to deflect the Social Security issue – which itself indicates an epic case of possible felony fraud – *not by trying to prove the allegation to be false and ridiculous, but rather by pointing out that, "Nothing in the Constitution makes even having a Social Security card or number a necessity to run for President!"*

In a 2012 New Jersey court, *the judge in the*

case, Jeff Masin, actually seemed to help Obama's lawyer, Alexandra Hill, stick to this strategy that because, as Judge Masin put it: *"The question of whether the document that is produced turns out to be a forgery, it seems to me is irrelevant because he hasn't produced it." Well, folks, what kind of logic is that judge trying to espouse?*

About 1981 at the age of 18, by way of Indonesia, Pakistan, Kenya, or Hawaii, Obama arrived in Chicago. And, from that time, Barack Obama and his actions reflect a murky and uncertain background. Actually, even with a *supposed fistful of degrees* from Columbia University and Princeton, he is best known for his background as a *community organizer* on the Southside of Chicago: advising and instructing *welfare* and *lower-income folks* on where and how to get food stamps, flu shots, and protest in offices of Section Eight Housing for cheap rent! And how to keep from getting caught using, or selling dope in addition to working to build an electoral campaign voting bloc base!

His Introduction and Formation of His Base and What Might Be Called His "Inner Circle"

And so, as a community organizer, Obama worked among his clientele on the Southside of Chicago, acquainting himself with folks such as Tony Rezko (*now in federal prison) who sold the mansion - Obama's home- to Obama,* at half-price*!*

Also, let's not forget the influence of the avowed Communist, Frank Marshall Davis, the founder of the Weather Underground, and radical terrorist, Bill Ayers, both of whom were also mentors of Obama.

There is considerable evidence of Iranian born Valerie Jarrett's influence on Obama's career. In a *Whistleblower* magazine issue, it describes how, when working for the city of Chicago, Ms. Jarrett hired Michelle Obama and gave the couple access to the exclusive world of "upper-class" black Chicago politics!

Now, let's try to keep this as simple as possible! Having become acquainted with Communist Frank Marshall Davis, Obama then met Iranian born, Valerie Jarrett, who he later chose as his Chief White House advisor! In her job for the

City of Chicago, Valerie Jarrett had met and hired Michelle Lavaughn Robinson, the future Michelle Obama*! (Now, get the picture).* Michelle had also worked at the Sidley Austin law firm, where the former FBI fugitive, Bernadine Dohrn *(*who was married to the radical Bill Ayers), also worked and Barack Hussein Obama got a summer job there.

So folks, what we have here is the group of *friends, tutors, mentors,* call them what you will, (Communists, Socialists, radicals, terrorists, and *Leaky Vessels),* who comprise Obama's *Inner Circle of conspirators and confidantes,* and who are responsible more than any other people, for the thoughts, attitudes, and directions of the guy we now have as *President of our Country,* sitting in the Oval Office! Once again, let's name them*!*

The Avowed Communist, Frank Marshall Davis

The Reverend Jeremiah **(goddam America)** Wright!

Tony Rezko, (now in federal prison) who sold the mansion (Obama's home) to Obama, at half-price.

The radical Weather Underground Terrorist, Bill Ayers

Former FBI Fugitive (wife of Bill Ayers), ***Bernadine Dohrn***

Leftist, Iranian born ***Valerie Jarrett****, who Obama later chose as his White House Advisor! (She continues in this capacity!)*

Obama's White grandparents who were members of the American Communist Party, having joined years before, while living in Seattle! (They remained members until their deaths.)

Van Jones*, an African American friend and former adviser in Obama's cabinet, and an affirmed Communist*

And, although we have to say speculative, there is a well-researched conclusion that ***Bill Ayers*** *is the foremost author of Obama's book, Dreams from My Father!*

David Axelrod was a driving force behind Obama, and was his campaign and political director as well as an advisor! But, as far as Axelrod being a member of Obama's inner circle, we can't truthfully say. Possibly, Axelrod was, or is, maybe, the best of a bad bunch!

This leaves the average person wondering: How does an 18-year old Obama, (even with his mother's *wanderlust life style* and his White grandparents in Hawaii being long-time members of the American Communist Party*),* arrive in Chicago in 1982, and through the next 15 years or so, align and immerse himself with not just one or two, but a complete *Inner Circle* of people who are all, on the seamy side of humanity, as terrorists, outright Communists, or both?

And ironically, although somewhat humorously, this makes us wonder as to whether these people, *Obama's Friends and Inner Circle,* with most of them considered Communists, radicals, Socialists, (the Garbage Dump Bunch*), or whatever*, would even be allowed to enter Russia, *a bono fide* Communist nation! *(Considering President Putin's very evident dislike of Obama, it would be doubtful)!*

There doesn't appear to be a single individual

in Obama's inner circle, who we would call, *a Patriotic American who loves this Country!* There are certain *Leaky Vessels* in his cabinet such as Susan Rice and Samantha Powers, who, even though naively close to Obama, are probably not a part of his *Deep Inner Circle! (And certainly, not Vice President Joe Biden)*!

But, as we realize from the above information, Obama's Inner Circle was formed during his early years in Chicago!

Well, let's take a more intense look at the background of President Obama! His father, Barack Obama, Sr., met Anne Dunham (Obama's mother) in Honolulu in 1960, and they were supposedly married in February, 1961. However, there doesn't seem to be any records of marriage licenses, etc., and maybe it doesn't matter! President Obama was born on August 4, 1961.

To repeat, in Hawaii, Anne Dunham met Barack Obama, Sr. from Kenya. It has been claimed they were married February 2, 1961 in Maui. However, *no marriage certificate has ever been seen and no witnesses were present at the supposed ceremony.*

Also, there is no evidence Barack Obama, Sr. and Ann Dunham ever lived together, sharing a common residence, or that he ever financially supported his supposedly new *'wife'*. *The date and place of the 'marriage' appears only in the divorce record. (Actually, he was already married to a lady from Kenya at that time)!* Barack Obama, Jr. was born August 4, 1961, (somewhere)!

During Obama's campaign for the 2008 presidential election he portrayed his mother as a conservative girl from Kansas; however in reality she was a radical Leftist and cultural Marxist. She lived in the Seattle area, spending her teenage years in Seattle's coffee shops with other young Leftist radicals. Obama claims that his mother's family were conservative Methodists or Baptists from Kansas. *Actually, his grandparents were members of a left-wing Unitarian church near Seattle. The church (located in Bellevue, Washington) was nicknamed "the little red church," because of its Communist leanings. They had joined the American Communist Party!*

Now, let's be honest! Trying to sort out President Obama's father's background (what he did, how many colleges he attended, how many wives -

supposedly six, with *eight kids*), well folks, President Obama's father's background, *(like his own)* is just a total mess, and probably, just ain't worth the effort it would take! But, concerning Obama's father, he was undoubtedly the world's worst automobile driver. After returning to Kenya at age 46, he was killed in his fourth car wreck, in 1982, by *ramming his pickup truck into a tree!* But, considering (let's say) his lifestyle of *screwing around and breeding kids*, if he had lived another 40 years, he would have re-populated the entire African continent!

It's said that Obama was 4 years old before his father saw him, just about the time that his mother, Anne Dunham, met Lolo Soetoro, who was from Indonesia. She ended up marrying Soetoro and moving to Indonesia, but after a short time, sent her son, *Barack,* to live with the White grandparents in Hawaii!

To reiterate, Obama's acquaintances and mentors were all *leaky vessels* such as Bill Ayers, founder and leader of the *Weather Underground*, the radical, terrorist organization, known for blowing up Federal buildings and killing several people in San Francisco and other places around the country! Now, this was *during and continuing after the years of the*

Vietnam War protests! Obama insists that he was eight years old when Bill Ayers was blowing up buildings and causing deaths around the country!

Well, maybe true! But he was around 20 years of age when he was really getting to become indoctrinated by Ayers. (The first fundraisers for Obama's election campaign for the Illinois State Senate were held in *Bill Ayer's Hyde Park home in Chicago!)* Also, Frank Marshall Davis, *the avowed Communist,* was part of the group, and *many of those who knew them, say that Davis is Obama's actual father,* however, we are not, *(repeat not)*, saying this is, by any means, true! We don't know and don't care. Possibly, DNA garnered from Obama and Davis would settle the allegations, if anyone does care!

Strangely, it doesn't seem that there is any evidence of Barack Obama, Sr. having ever met Anne Dunham, President Obama's mother prior to four months before her giving birth to Obama on August 4th, 1961.

And, with evidence indicating that Obama, Sr. was already married to a woman in Kenya, we also found no evidence that Obama, Sr. had been engaged to or lived together with Anne Dunham. From what we could discern, the two did not live together before or after being married, and there were no letters, ring, announcements or, most importantly, no legal marriage registration with the State of Hawaii.

It does appear that Anne Dunham was granted a statutory divorce from Obama, Sr. in Hawaii in 1964 b*ut court documents show no original documented proof of the two ever being married, or, any legal documents showing Obama, Sr. as the father of Anne Dunham's child* ... (Little Barack)!

Michelle, Obama, and Axelrod's Medical Clinics

Early on, or about 1996, before Obama had been elected to the Illinois State Senate, Michelle Obama was in charge of patient admittance at the University of Chicago Hospital Clinic, (UCMC). But she saw possibilities and created a program that actually *steered away* low-income (Medicaid) patients seeking admittance and treatment at the University of Chicago Clinic where she was employed.

She steered them to other medical clinics, *mainly, the Urban Health Initiative* clinics in which she *(Michelle),* Barack Obama, and David Axelrod, had a special interest! These clinics had been set up to serve the *Obama's Southside Chicago area!* They were supposedly funded by Illinois State grants which had been garnered by the then *new State Senator, Barack Obama!*

Earlier, David Axelrod, who had joined the Obamas (being introduced and brought into the group by Michelle), was a strong force in helping Obama get elected to the Illinois State Senate! And, if our information is correct, it is at this time that the controversial Bill Ayers, had joined the group, hosting Obama's first fundraiser at his (Ayers) home!

In the early days of the year 2009, if I remember correctly, there was information on the Internet (Google, etc.) that there were five medical clinics which had been set up and financed by an eleven million dollar grant which had been obtained from the State of Illinois by then, Illinois State Senator Barack Obama! *Accordingly, the Obamas, David Axelrod, and Valerie Jarrett, are partners in the clinics and enterprises.*

If memories are correct, the now called, *Urban Health Initiative* clinics were first installed as the *Southside Health Collaborative* clinics and were renamed and changed to the *Urban Health Imitative* clinics because the original name sounded too much like a *"Chicago Southside po' folks"* operation, and so, the name change!

The above referenced clinics are now called the Urban Health Initiative clinics and were installed to serve *low income Medicaid patients!* And, of course, most were sent over from the UCMC by Michelle, to the appreciation of the Obamas (Michelle and Barack), Valerie Jarrett, and David Axelrod, all partners and owners of the now called, Urban Health Initiative clinics!

The following article *(lifted from the Internet)*

is actually a reinforcement of the above information! *You can form your own opinion if interested! As follows...*Quote:

> "The First Lady helped create a notorious program that dumped poor patients on community hospitals, yet the national media ignored the story as they always do when the Obamas are the focus!
>
> The University of Chicago Medical Center has received a good deal of justly opprobrious press over its *policy of 'redirecting' low-income patients to community hospitals while reserving its own beds for well-heeled patients requiring highly profitable procedures.* Substantial coverage was given to a recent indictment of the program by the American College of Emergency Physicians. ACEP's president, Dr. Nick Jouriles, released a statement suggesting that the initiative comes *dangerously close to 'patient dumping,' a practice made illegal by the Emergency Medical Labor and Treatment Act, and reflected an effort to 'cherry pick' wealthy patients over the poor."*

Now, not to confuse, our view is, that the *"dumping of patients"* was to *acquire* low income Medicaid patients so as to g*enerate money and profits* for Michelle and her partners, Barack Obama, David Axelrod, and Valerie Jarett (who I believe to be the owners of the now-called Urban Health Initiative), rather than the Chicago Hospital-UCMC-where she worked.

Now, let us say, that the acquisition and building of these clinics was effected back in the year of 2008, and if the Obamas and the individuals listed above *were* not, and *are* not the owners, *we would be very happy to apologize!*

Further, if one wonders just why the Chicago crime rate is so extremely high, the following is one good example of the causes!

It was probably around 1994 when the Chicago Public Housing Authority experimented with the "Midnight Basketball" scenario, spending millions building *basketball courts* in the hope that teenagers, instead of causing mischief, would instead, play basketball during the late night hours. Of course, this would (and did) prevent them from rising early, being alert, attending school and getting an education! *No doubt, that these young (mostly Black) folks will end up uneducated and stupid, but maybe they won't steal or riot and cause problems!*

By checking the felony arrest percentages and the murder rate within the age bracket of those former *teen-aged basketball players*, it would more than likely, reflect the almost certain consequences of an obviously moronic program! If I am correct, Chicago has the reputation as the murder capital of America, especially with *Black Americans* killing

Black Americans! It would seem that *the Reverend Al Sharpton and our Attorney General, Eric Holder, could be used there (not to attempt to inflame racial tensions), but to try to stop the Black on Black crime that is so prevalent in the inner city and the Southside areas of Chicago!*

A No-Bid Healthcare.gov-Contract

Just recently, rumors are beginning to surface about the terribly flawed Obama's Healthcare Contract, which are to say, at the least, disturbing. Are the rumors true? Here's the story!

First Lady Michelle Obama's Princeton classmate Toni Townes-Whitley is a top executive at the company that *received the no-bid contract* to build the failed Obamacare website! Ms. Townes-Whitley, Princeton class of '85, is a senior vice president at CGI Federal, which somehow, received the *no-bid contract to build the $678 million Obamacare enrollment website at* <u>Healthcare.gov</u>. (CGI Federal is the U.S. arm of a Canadian company)!

Michelle Obama and her Princeton classmate, Townes-Whitley are both members of the Association of the Black Princeton Alumni.

Toni Townes-Whitley, is a onetime policy

analyst with the General Accounting Office and previously served in the Peace Corps in Gabon, West Africa. Her decision to return to work as an African-American woman after six years of raising kids, was applauded by a Princeton alumni publication in 1998.

George Schindler, the president for the U.S. and Canada of the Canadian-based CGI Group, CGI Federal's parent company, *became an Obama 2012 campaign donor after his company gained the Obamacare website contract.*

On the government end, construction of the disastrous Healthcare.gov website was overseen by the Centers for Medicare and Medicaid Services (CMS), a division of longtime failed website-builder Kathleen Sibelius' Department of Health and Human Services.

So, we draw these important conclusions:

1. It was a no-bid contract, with no American companies considered;

2. A designated Canadian company received the contract!

Barack Obama's 2008 Presidential Campaign

(News Media Coverage and Protection)

(Since about 1959, most of us have been admirers and background supporters of our space program. We were proud when President Kennedy enabled our USA efforts to immediately equal the Russians in putting up our first "Sputnik". Sadly, the new US President, Barack Obama, in 2009, cancelled our space program and our people have since been paying taxi fare to Russia for a ride to the Space Shuttle! Just thought you would like to know!)

In 2007, due to a number of factors, such as the popular talk show host, Oprah Winfrey, introducing and accompanying him into the early presidential primary of the state of Iowa, he was able to overcome the candidacy of Hillary Clinton. With that said, national news networks (ABC, CBS, and NBC, already swooning over Obama, potentially the first Black president of the United States), climbed into bed with him, and gave him a free ride with zero background investigation known as vetting, which is, normally, a proper part of the public's right and need to know! So, this was a disgrace and Obama won the Iowa primary.

A failure by the major news networks (including CNN and MSNBC), sadly, they still continue to function in the *Protect Obama Mode.*

Thoughts and Opinions of the News Media

Concerning the background of both President Obama and his *(maybe)* father, Obama, Sr., in almost anyone's learned opinion, Chris Matthews, Ed Schultz, and the Squirrels over at the "Squirrel Cage" (MSNBC), should have spent more time investigating Barack Obama and his father's background, and less time ignoring or trying to cover it up! And while we're on the subject, there has never been any doubt about MSNBC's, Ed Schultz's feelings about Obama! He has referred to Obama as *A man that I love*!

Now, most viewers would question, *and rightly so*, as to whether Schultz, who would never think of giving a truthful news report in which Obama (a man that Schultz loves) was mentioned somewhat unfavorably, should be allowed to actually report news on any news network *(even with zero ratings)* such as *MSNBC!*

Here are just a couple of observations or questions on which Ed Schultz and Chris Matthews could engage and shed some light. Consider the following:

President Obama is running around the world on endless vacations with crowds of people in his entourage, and costing hundreds of millions of dollars, not to mention the first Lady Michelle, on separate trips with multitudes in her entourage, and always staying in the most expensive and luxurious accommodations! Such was her recent trip to China where she stayed at one of China's most expensive hotels with exorbitant rates; then there's the resort near Barcelona, Spain, with a huge entourage requiring 60 rooms at, we are told, a rate of $2500 nightly per room and staying for a week!

And even when she vacations with her husband, President Obama, she travels separately, requiring additional Air Force planes, helicopters and staff. Of course, her educational tour to South Africa *(costing millions),* paid off *big time,* where she is highly visible, teaching the South African kids *how to play hopscotch! (And not a GOP Congressman or Senator with enough balls to even mention and oppose this very foolish widespread waste)!*

We take note of the fact and wonder why, on one of his very few trips to Africa President Obama has never stopped in Kenya and paid at least a token visit to his father's and grandparents' home, and at least said *Howdy* to some of his many relatives. Heaven knows, with his father's reputation of *"screwing around, (fanning the cover so to speak) and having kids",* Obama could for the first time, meet and greet some of his many *kinfolks! In other words, enjoy* a *small family reunion.*

(*By comparison, President George W. Bush and the First Lady Laura Bush vacationed mostly at his ranch in Crawford, Texas where the accommodations were free).*

Did Obama Arm the Terrorist Group Hamas? Deliberately, Naively, or Coincidentally?

In an article of a late issue of *Time Magazine*, (August 25th, 2014) it is pretty well made clear that the terror group, Hamas, was birthed and is owned by the *radical Muslim Brotherhood,* which seems to be President Obama's special step-child! And this brings into play a completely new vein of thought which unveils a good question that needs to be answered, such as: *Why was President Obama so intent on the destruction of President Mubarak of Egypt and the overthrow of his government, thereby fomenting problems and discord among the populace during a so-called Arab Spring uprising?*

Was it pure coincidence that Obama had the *Muslim Brotherhood* with its leader, Mohamed Morsi, waiting in the wings, to swiftly come into power in Egypt during the *Arab Spring* and the so-called Democratic elections? And, of course, made possible by the purposeful bombings and destruction of the Egyptian government orchestrated by the actions of President Obama and his pawn, Secretary of State Hillary Clinton. This, of course, all helped to make possible the easy and swift installation of Morsi, **the leader of the Muslim Brotherhood**, as President of Egypt!

The evident stupidity of Obama and Hillary went even further with President Obama, immediately after Morsi's election as President of Egypt, giving a large number of our F-16 fighter jets, plus **One Point Five Billion Dollars** of the American taxpayer's money to Morsi and his Muslim Brotherhood! We were then thanked by the Muslim Brotherhood's burning and destroying our Embassy in Cairo, at the approximate time that Al Qaida was ransacking our Embassy and killing our Ambassador and personnel in Libya, during the Benghazi incident!

And, after that incident, the deliberate lying and fairy tales, such as trying to place the blame on a Youtube movie which supposedly offended Muslims, allegedly made by an individual who Obama called *a kind of a shadowy person!* And, the very obvious rehearsed lying by President Obama, Susan Rice, and Secretary of State Hillary Clinton! (As actors, each would have been nominated for an Oscar)!

(Of course, hardly any Muslims had even seen or heard of the so-called movie).

Were those events just coincidental or related? Well, consider, - as has been said -, that most of the terror groups are sort of kinfolks or kissing cousins with mutual goals, and inevitably we have to ask the question: *By what good reason did we attack Libya, causing us to be there in the first place? Also, - and in no way understandable - Hillary Clinton has recently laid the blame for the problems and discord in the Mideast on (you guessed it) Israel!*

Now, it is important to note, as to the question above, it has been reported, although very quietly, that part of the finances used by Hamas to build tunnels (used by the Hamas terrorists to covertly enter into Israel, buy arms, and commit atrocities, etc., against Israel) came from the **One Point Five Billion Dollars** which was, very foolishly, given to the Muslim Brotherhood by President Barack Obama.

Now, here is something to think about! If Obama, by furnishing the finances to the *Muslim Brotherhood, (Hamas),* and those finances being used by the *Hamas terrorists* to buy the arms, etc., that were used to attack Israel, would it not follow that, in any common sense court of law, Obama would be judged an accessory, or an accomplice? As in *furnishing the driver and the car used in a bank robbery?*

However, as we wrote in the John McCain chapter, even the Egyptians couldn't stomach Obama and Morsi's Muslim Brotherhood, throwing them out of power in Egypt after a short time, with new elections and electing a far more sensible and moderate President Abdel Fattah el-Sisi! But during the brief time the Muslim Brotherhood was in power, Egypt's Peace Accord with Israel, which we remember was set into place by Jimmy Carter about 35 years ago, was dissolved by the Brotherhood.

A few months ago, our great and wonderful Secretary of State, John Kerry, was in the process of handing over $212 Million of American taxpayer dollars to the Palestinians. And of course, the Muslim Brotherhood, Hamas, and the Palestinians are all intertwined (kissing cousins), with each other, so this extra "Kerry Cash" will help buy more arms and weapons for Hamas to use in attacking Israel!

A late note: As we've said before, in our opinion, it's pretty hard for *Time Magazine* contributor Joe Klein to consistently walk a straight path of reality *and* truth while at the same time trying to paint a positive picture of Obama's senseless, devastating actions in Egypt and the Mideast! And, also to join in these actions by his then Secretary of State, Hillary Clinton!

Having said this, Klein, in writing a far more moderate and sensible article in a recent *Time's* issue (January 11, 2015), almost had to contradict himself when he wrote of a possible conciliatory attitude between Saudi Arabia, Egypt, and Israel. Abdel Fattah el-Sisi, President of Egypt, is quoted in a speech on New Year's Day as saying in essence, *It makes no sense that our thoughts which we hold sacred, should cause the entire Islamic world to be a source of danger, killing, and destruction for the rest of the world.*

Now, we must remind ourselves that Mr. Abdel Fattah el-Sisi was elected President in Egypt after the overthrow of Obama's buddies, Morsi and his Muslim Brotherhood. Of course, let's remember that President Obama's agenda which caused the devastation in Egypt, Libya, and throughout the Mideast, also was ardently supported by Joe Klein! I must say that I don't recall writer Joe Klein ever objecting to Obama's policies and actions. He has ardently supported all of Obama's agenda in the Mideast, an agenda which has been proven to be totally dangerous and amateurish! In earlier editions and articles, Klein termed Obama's policies and actions concerning Egypt, Libya, and the Mideast as, *"Right Every Time"*!

Trivial Crap from the News Media

Thankfully, there are some reporters who, without doubt, stand apart from let's say, Matt Lauer, Bryan Williams, Scott Pelley, Diane Sawyer, and the rest of the "generic bunch"! Two fine examples of dedication to truth and expertise are Lara Logan and Cheryl Atkinson. It appears Chery Atkinson was so truthful and competent that her employer (CBS) terminated her! More about both of them later.

As is often said, no one familiar with the field of journalism would ever boast that journalists and reporters are generally *extra smart* people! Sure, they look impressive in a $2,000.00 suit! But we can wonder in awe and ask just how a Chris Matthews or Candy Crowley and other news network stars seem to wear *blinders to the point of being totally naive*! And never realized, or informed their audience, the American people, as to the *real* Obama, his background, his associates, or intentions. Well, the answer would simply be, *"Naiveté"!*

A huge amount of *trivial crap* is shoveled out to viewers as "breaking news or main stories" in order to fill up newscasts and ignore more important world or national news which might be unfavorable to Obama or the Democratic administration. This makes for a less informed public, and is part of the *Protect Obama Mode*! Here are some good examples of how the network news shows promote *and* magnify *fluff* or *trivia news,* and downplay, or gloss over, important news and downplay or gloss over important news:

For an example, a typical opening major lead story featured on the NBC Today show might be, "Breaking News! Aunt Sarah Bennett, 91, has been acclaimed the winner in the Aunt Dinah Quilting contest in Eutaw, Texas, a contest dating back to the year of 1882. Aunt Sarah, the clear winner, was the overall favorite and received an extra-large piece of party cake, and a small glass of homemade blackberry wine! She says she feels like the age of 60 again"! Interviews with Sarah, her daughter, two granddaughters and her four great-granddaughters, all coming up on NBC. Stay tuned!

"Also, with *Russia's President Putin* displaying his *always obvious contempt of President Obama*, a

U.S. destroyer was fired upon and severely damaged by a Russian torpedo off the coast of Ukraine last night, causing multiple deaths! Whether the attack was intentional is not known! Time permitting, we'll get back to that, plus, exciting breakthroughs on health tips, dieting, makeup, Hollywood celebrity arrests, and of course, plenty of giggles, all coming up on NBC, so stay with us!"

On ABC's Good Morning America, the show might open with, *"Breaking News, our top story,* 12 year-old Little Billy Hickcock won the annual *Amateur Goat Roping* contest last night in Wahoo, Nebraska. Little Billy walked over to the judge's stand with a real *Cowboy Swagger* and accepted his $25.00 prize and promised the crowd of 350 people a big slice of goat barbecue! Interviews with Billy, his grandfather, father, mother and six sisters later in the show!

Also, last night, Iran tested and detonated two nuclear bomb blasts, coupled with a warning to Israel to 'dismiss any and all claims to Palestinian lands.' When asked for comments, President Obama said that "Secretary of State John Kerry would *be issuing a stern rebuttal to the Iranian Prime Minister within the next three months or so"!*

It would not be surprising to hear either of the networks, CBS, NBC, or ABC News, to issue a statement such as:

"Our late surveys reveal that *hard negative news* tends to depress viewers, so henceforth, we have decided to stop reporting any real hard news which might be considered negative, so we welcome you to our new *positive feel good programming*! It's all coming up, including our brand new feature segment, *Giggle Fest*! So stay with us! And, although *we would strongly discourage such a move, in fairness, we might invite those who prefer to live in the real world and view all news, good and bad, to turn to one of the cable news sources such as Fox News!*"

This reminds us that we might call for a round of applause for two possibly former CBS reporters who went beyond the call of duty and actually reported the news *and* truth! We remember the CBS reporter Lara Logan from South Africa who had her clothes torn off and was raped repeatedly by men in the crowd in Tahrir Square in Cairo, Egypt. The crowd was celebrating the victory over President Mubarak, *whose down-fall was caused by the sustained bombings and attacks from the U.S., which were set in motion by the actions of Obama and Secretary of State, Hillary Clinton!*

Lara Logan told her story with video which was shown on *60 Minutes* and hosted by Scott Pelley. And we also remember Scott Pelley, in closing, saying in his sonorous, funeral type voice, *and we will never know whether it was the regime or the celebrating victors who were responsible!*

But clearly, that was not Mubarak's people in that crowd! It was composed of the *Muslim Brotherhood!* Let's not forget that *Obama and Secretary of State Hillary Clinton were 100 percent responsible for ending the thirty years plus peace agreement between Egypt and Israel!*

While we can't read Scott Pelley's mind, I would think that old Scott was carefully trying to orchestrate a "share the blame" and infer that some of Mubarak's military could have participated in the rapes of Lara Logan! *But as we said, that crowd was without doubt not Mubarak's military regime, which was on the run, but was made up of the celebrating Muslim Brotherhood!*

All things considered, let's award *Good Ole Scott Pelley* the dubious honor of membership in the *Washington Weasels Association*!

Also, Ms. Cheryl Atkinson who gave a much needed truthful exposé on the Benghazi fiasco has reportedly been expunged from the CBS News after 20 years and several Grammys, and was certainly a shining light of CBS, and, along with Lara Logan, the best of CBS!

(A special and vital input by former CBS News investigative reporter Cheryl Atkinson says that CBS News executives kept a clip of President Obama's refusing to call the Benghazi attacks terrorism, secret until after the election in order to help his re-election).

As this book was being written, 276 school girls in Nigeria have been captured by Boko Haram, a terrorist group in Nigeria. After multiple days of almost tearful expressions of hashtags and sympathy, Obama finally said that Nigeria is a sovereign nation and that we - the United States - were not able to interfere without an invitation!

A question: It makes one wonder about **Egypt,** which had a peace - pact with **Israel** for 30 years, and was a buffer between Israel and the Palestinians! Being attacked by the U.S. with bombs and missiles - *without any declaration of war* - for days or weeks and having Egypt's entire government and military destroyed by Obama, Hillary Clinton, and their regime, *well, the question: Was Egypt a sovereign nation?*

Ramblins ...!

(It's nice to have this space to offer some opinions, along with some interesting articles that would not be included if we did not believe the information offered was, for the most part, true! However, even with some of the writings being speculative and lacking 100% accuracy, they should perk the interest)!

News Magazine, Time, Etc.

Let's talk briefly about news magazines: *Time, Newsweek, US News and World Report*, etc. Some of these magazines have been around longer than most of the readers. This begs the question: Why do some magazines continue to publish and stay in business and others either belly-up or slim their operations down to the point of just barely staying alive?

For example, *Newsweek*. Most of the pundits say that over a period of time *Newsweek* became so liberal with its editorial and news content that readership numbers dropped and advertising revenue dried up! And so, inevitably came the end of

Newsweek, a formerly fine magazine.

I was a subscriber to *Time Magazine* for about 15 years until the viewpoints and writings of the columnists grew consistently so left-wing and zany, I dropped my subscription a few years ago (2011). Many of us knew that the editor Richard Stengel was a nice guy, but a left-winger and a "leaky vessel" and that *Time* was owned by NBC and the New York Times, etc. One could almost feel the magazine going downhill, and sure enough, a few months later, a pretty, and I believe, smart lady, Ms. Nancy Gibbs, was named Editor of *Time*. Somehow, there is a *gut feeling* that she was given the job of trying to restore the good quality and integrity of *Time*. I have recently renewed my subscription.

We want to wish Nancy and her folks good luck with *Time*. And quite frankly, Nancy, if you would entertain the idea of changing locations and moving your editorial staff, writers, contributors, and complete publishing operations to, let's say, Fort Worth, Texas, I believe that your entire group would benefit and be endowed with a greater knowledge, understanding and *feel* of the real world! *Time* would have a totally new and refreshing image with that *Texas Flavor of Truth*, and just to move out of the

New York City environment would be a blessing! After all, there *ain't* many folks who can hang around New York City very long and still think with a sound mind and a clear head!

And, thinking further, it might be a good idea to bring along the *New York Times* with its editorial staff and writers! After all, we know the continually warped and liberal Democratic or Republican thinking normally displayed in the *Times,* is not because of those writers having been born with such DNA! Rather, it's derived from the *long-time close association with people of like thought!* With the *New York Times* moving its operations to Fort Worth, and with its writers and staff given a couple of weeks to clear their heads of New York City smog and Pentothal, we could rejoice in the difference.

And, then there is the talented *New York Times* ladies such as Maureen Dowd! I believe these ladies would flourish in a Fort Worth, Texas, atmosphere, with Texas cowboys and rednecks, like myself. Being used to the rude pushing and shoving in New York City, I believe those ladies would find it refreshing when going into a restaurant or getting on an elevator in Fort Worth, for a Texas cowboy to bow, tip his hat, smile, and say, *After you, ma'am!*

This is not to say that there are not several fine writers in the *Time* enclave! Earlier in this book, I mentioned that I was a fan of Michael Scherer; also Michael Crowley, Rana Foroohar and others.

However, Fareed Zakaria does appear to need help. In one fairly recent article concerning the prosperity and development of some very small nations, he stated that the *Nationalist Chinese had been abandoned on Taiwan by the world* and still became a small country of prosperity. *Truthfully, multitudes of Chinese* had fled from the Chinese mainland and Mongolia to Taiwan (*Formosa then*), along with the former leader of China, Chiang Kai-shek, in the late 1940's. But, they were in no sense, *abandoned*!

Rather than being *abandoned, they were protected for years by the routine patrols of the U.S. Navy's Seventh Fleet blockade of the Formosa Straits in order to prevent any incursions from Mao Tse-tung and his Communist rule on the mainland!* And, further, both Taipei, the capital of Formosa, and the City of Kao-chung on the southern coast, were large cities with modern hotels and restaurants, with a large Catholic mission in Taipei. There were U.S. Naval bases and military establishments, both in Taipei and Kao-chung, and this protection and friendship endured for years. I was a second class Petty Officer aboard the *USS Cacapon,* and we were in and out of Taipei and Kao-chung, Formosa during those years.

(No big deal, Fareed ... Just a little research should take care of this and future allegations. Good luck always)!

More Ramblins - Gay Marriage Thoughts

A few days ago, several of my neighbors stopped by and were allowed to look at a few pages of my book. One asked if I had included any opinions at all on gays and gay marriage. I said *no.* When asked why, I said. *I don't care,* which is true.

While the idea of a gay lifestyle is abhorrent to most of us, I do think that whatever *melts their butter* is fine with me. I think as far as lifestyles are concerned, I have to believe that when people mind their own business and are good neighbors, they, and we as citizens, are all subject to the same laws and privileges.

However, there are some people, such as members of the ACLU for instance, who often claim to be offended by a Nativity presentation on a courthouse lawn and go to great lengths to have it removed. Well, those particular *ACLU- SOB's* offend me, so I would like to try to personally remove a few of them!

It seems that the subject of gay marriage is used to a large degree by some politicians who mistakenly believe that an election platform of *coming out and opposing gays being allowed to marry,* will get them elected! *(Wrong, most of the time)*!

On the other hand, openly exhorting or

promoting gay marriage will more than likely get them defeated!

But, admittedly, the gay community is responsible to a large degree, for the attention and animosity towards their group. *Gay Pride Day* parades, for instance, with crowds of buffoons and clowns marching, holding up signs and flags, and singing, *"Hey, look at me, I'm gay. I was born at an early age and just grew up funny this way!"*

It causes one to think, "We don't want to be bothered with the subject, so shut up, go home, and we promise not to tell anyone"! Good advice to Will and Bill would be to, "Mind your own business, and keep it to yourselves!"

Members of the Washington Weasels Association

As it is certainly understood, space and time do not permit us to discuss or even mention all the individuals in Washington who serve in important positions in government and deserve membership as *Weasels*. Here are a few of the more prominent, recognizable names of individuals and well-known journalists, writers and news media who we believe are most surely deserving of membership in the *Washington Weasels Association*, as follows:

QUALIFIED WEASELS

Rachel Maddow	*MSNBC*	The Squirrel Cage
Candy Crowley	*CNN News*	Far out Liberal
Debbie Wasserman Schultz	*Democrat*	Far out Liberal
Susan Rice	*Cabinet Member*	Far out Liberal
Nancy Pelosi	*Member of Congress*	Far out Liberal
Valerie Jarrett	*Obama Advisor*	Far out Liberal
Chris Matthews	*MSNBC*	The Squirrel Cage
Ed Schultz	*MSNBC*	The Squirrel Cage
Charlie Gibson	*ABC News Anchor*	Destroyed his own credibility while attempting to destroy Sarah Palin with a "gotcha" question! Star Member of *The Washington Weasels Association*
Bryan Williams	*NBC News Anchor (currently on extended leave for fabricating a story)*	Liberal and biased; traveled with and carried the banner for Obama during 2012 presidential election, and appeared to be totin' Obama's luggage and teleprompter
Joe Klein	*Writer for Time Magazine*	Extremely liberal
David Brooks	*New York Times and PBS News Hour*	Extremely liberal RINO

Some Believable and Respected Individuals

There are so many hundreds of worthy people that we would love to include in the "Most Admired" group, but sadly, space just doesn't permit. However, we couldn't leave without mentioning some people who I believe, are a blessing to this country. Thanks to you all!

Charlie Rose	*CBS and PBS*	Despite being a part of the liberal news media environment, I believe Charlie Rose might ignore or gloss over substantive facts, but somehow, I don't believe Charlie would lie.
Judy Woodruff	*PBS*	She seems to be a straight shooter and does a great job of "holding their feet to the fire" during interviews! Judy, I believe, does not lie.
Bob Schaeffer	*CBS News*	Is a pretty good fellow I think, and let's cut him a little slack. I don't believe he's much of a liar. (He's also a pretty good country singer)
Gwen Ifield	*PBS*	A straight shooter. We can like her, and we can trust her!
Al Roker	*NBC*	We can like Al and we can trust him, especially when he talks about the weather!
Megan Kelley	*FOX NEWS*	We can like and believe this lady!

Patrick Buchanan		Well-known stalwart conservative and straight shooter
Michael Scherer	*Writer for Time Magazine*	A solid believable writer
Jake Tapper	*NBC News*	A pretty solid guy
Natalie Morales	*NBC "Today Show"..*	Even being immersed in a totally unbelievable network, I believe Natalie is a solid reporter. I would think that we can trust her.
Savannah Guthrie	*NBC - The Today Show.*	Surprisingly believable
George Stephanopoulos	*ABC News*	After years with Bill Clinton, and called by some as the *"Little Boy Who Never Grew Up"*, George is for the most part, a pretty solid guy.
Bill O'Reilly Britt Hume Charles Krauthammer	*Fox Cable News*	… and all the folks at Fox Cable News; trustworthy, and especially needed
Michael Scherer	*Time Magazine*	A solid, believable writer
Norah O'Donnell and Gail King, together with Charlie Rose	*CBS*	These three are capable of hosting a dynamite news show.

But for the most part, like NBC, and ABC, CBS is nothing more than an information outlet serving up dieting, exercise, school activities, fashions, and rarely, the *real news* that we need and are hungry for! So, Fox News Channel is the last resort.

Epilogue

In closing, a word of thanks to those who have bought or read this book. There will be some disagreement and some who will feel offended, but I wanted to write a book that was well-researched, and to the best of my ability, factual with substance. The larger part of the material is derived from memory. Now, I admit that there was, and is, a great difficulty in trying to discern and sort out the background of President Obama.

The Arizona Sheriff Joe Arpaio has probably conducted the most official and extensive investigation into Obama's history and birth, but he is stymied due to Arizona's attorney general being a Democrat. Sheriff Arpaio is also currently trying to deal with Obama's immigration policies. I also realize that I haven't been very complimentary in speaking of President Obama. And, that's true. Fortunately, his record speaks for itself.

Even though Obama's U.S. citizenship was not clearly documented, the total support and naiveté of our news media (NBC, ABC, and CBS) helped usher him into the Presidency of the most prestigious, prosperous and stalwart nation on earth, the United States of America! But, sadly, even the great strengths and the strong fabric of the U.S. have been damaged and torn because of the policies and actions of Obama and his minions! We can only imagine the consequences of an Obama ruling and attempting to govern and manage one of the countries in Africa, of which none, have any semblance of solidarity of government in the first place!

We are told that about 90 million people are suffering under conditions of poverty, and quite naturally, none of us should be satisfied where any individual or demographic is unable to live and enjoy a decent and quality life. However, it would be of interest - and maybe useful - to look back and compare *living under today's poverty* to the real poverty that existed in the1930's! *And there are still a few of us who can do that!*

And, looking back, it does seem that today's so-called poverty tends to *pale* in comparison to the hard times of being just *plain po' folks back in the years of the 1930's and early 1940's.* Those were days and years of hard times that people were enduring.

Almost all folks were struggling to live and survive. There was very little money, *no food stamps, no Social Security! I was just a kid in those days, but I remember uncles and cousins (grown men) coming back home to their parents homes and farms because their manufacturing jobs in the big cities had ended.* And so, they came back home to live and work around the farms and to wait out the Depression! (Working in the fields paid about $2.00

per day)!

Since we were farmers, we always had enough to eat, although our diets were, *let's say,* simple. Lots of *Black-eyed peas, collard greens, and "sweet taters"*! About twice a month, Mama used to go out to the hen house and *"wring a neck or two" for fried chicken on Sunday!*

And how about electricity? Well, no one had electricity, and never thought about it. With no electricity and five of us kids (I had four sisters) we helped Mama to draw water from the 62-foot deep well for household use and to wash all our clothes! And, of course, without electricity and no running water, all of us country folks had an outhouse out back! And hey, there's nothing to be ashamed of in talking about outhouses. As I've believed and mentioned in my autobiography, we would all be better off and have a cleaner environment, if outhouses were mainly used across our country as do the Mennonites and the Quakers! Or at least, before the EPA bureaucrats began to meddle in Oklahoma, Ohio, and Pennsylvania!

But the problem of "toilet paper"! Nobody in those days ever used store-bought toilet paper or had any money to buy it even if it had been available! So, what to do? As I said earlier, this may not be a topic to discuss around the dinner table, but overall this is a book of truth and *arguably,* rich in substance! Well, the Sears Roebuck catalogs were widely distributed in those days and so, *Sears to the rescue!* Just about every outhouse was equipped with a catalog.

As we said earlier, folks in those days had no television or electric lights. Just coal oil lamps and a battery powered radio, and so, they went to bed early. As a result, there was a lot of time for *"fanning the cover"* and families grew large. While families having from five to eight kids was common, one of our neighbor's families had thirteen kids! So, how about an *extra catalog* and a round of applause for Sears?

Reminiscing with feelings of nostalgia, as a teenager of years gone past I remember standing outside of our country farmhouse in the fall and early winters of those years - let's say, through the 1950s - when flocks of geese would be flying over for days and days with their mournful honks and cries. And also flocks of ducks, all flying South! But sadly, seldom do we hear and see those marvelous, beautiful birds to the same extent as back then! Why are they disappearing? I don't know! I think that we are all in our hearts "animal rights" activists, but without the hypocrisy. And let me explain.

Back some 25 years ago, I had inherited the old country home in East Texas that had been owned by my Grandmother and had been built in the year of 1918. The old house sat on pilings and stood almost two feet off the ground in places. I moved from living in Las Vegas to the old home in East Texas, liked it and have lived here since! After I had lived here for about six months, I became aware that there were at least two skunks living under the house and from the movements and grunting I assumed they were just doing the normal functions of getting ready to raise a family of little "skunk kitties"! The skunks actually grew quite friendly and openly played around me in the yard at times. We always called them *pole cats* when I was growing up.

Anyway, regarding the animal rights activists, I had met an attractive lady in the town of Longview, Texas, about 10 miles away, and thought that I might get to know her a little faster by inviting her to be my guest for a weekend. (And with luck, a little *heavy courtin'*). To my surprise, she accepted, saying that she loved animals and country living, was an animal rights activist at heart, and that she would really enjoy it! And of course, have it understood that she didn't normally do things on short acquaintance like this.

Well, the first evening at dusk, we had enjoyed a light supper and were having a nice conversation. Just about that time, a series of grunts, groans, jolts, and bumping, started underneath the house. My new lady friend and guest looked sort of startled and asked me what the noises were. I told her simply that there was a large family of skunks living under the house, but they were friendly and just engaging in a some normal family courtin', and nothing to be bothered about! I expected a few "oohs and aahs", but no such luck!

The very next thing I knew, she was picking up her overnight bag, her purse and coat, and was opening the door! I asked her what was going on and she said, *I forgot I have a previous commitment for tonight, and have to go*! I asked her, *What's the problem*? She just said, *"Thank you, and I'm sorry"!* She went straight to her car, slammed the door and roared off down the road! So much for pretending to be an animal rights activist! *And she was such a nice lady, too!*

Of course, most of the animal rights activists are for the most part, sincere and dedicated, but some Rednecks and Republicans are saying that even though some women in the Democratic Party and Obama's Cabinet may have heard about the Spotted Owl, most of them are so dumb they think a Woodpecker is a decoy!

But those were times with prices that seem unbelievable now; coffee about 25 cents a pound, gasoline approximately 20 cents per gallon, and a bottle of Coca Cola or Pepsi Cola, 5 cents a bottle. But, the Japanese attacked Pearl Harbor in December, 1941, and World War II came along. Our country survived, prospered, and grew out of the Great Depression.

And now, thanks again to you for inviting me into your home through this book. In reaching out in goodwill, friendship, and harmony, I would like to pass along a treasured recipe from Aunt Sarah Bennett, who, as you remember, won the *Aunt Dinah Quilting Contest*! It seems that Aunt Sarah is not only a fine seamstress but a Queen in the kitchen as well when cooking *Southern Style!*

Several ladies who have used the recipe say that it is a most requested item for their Sunday Dinner.

(This recipe was forwarded on to me from a fine lady, Mrs. Lillian Richardson, in Silsbee, Texas.)

Aunt Sarah's Chicken and Apple Dumplings

INGREDIENTS:

Two	Red Delicious apples
Two	Cans of Crescent rolls (8 each)
Two	Sticks melted butter
8	Slices of pre-cooked chicken
2 tsp	Vanilla extract
2 tsp	Sugar
10 oz.	Apple juice
	Cinnamon to taste

Slice each apple into 8 slices, micro-wave for 2 minutes; Roll a slice of chicken and apple into each Crescent roll. Place in pan; pour mixture of melted butter, sugar, vanilla and cinnamon over rolls. Pour 10 oz. apple juice over rolls and bake at 350 degrees for 30 minutes; Cover loosely with foil, and bake an additional ten minutes. Serve! Prepare for a heartfelt round of applause!

In closing, let us say in our prayers, that as a country, there will hopefully be a great bonding and coming together! And, as the late and great Martin Luther King might say, "*And, one of these days, we're gonna climb that mountain and walk up there amongst them clouds, where the cotton's high and the corn's a growin'... and they ain't no fields to plow"!*

Ladies and Gentlemen, God Bless!

Claude Gray